THE WORKS OF SHAKESPEARE

EDITED FOR THE SYNDICS OF THE
CAMBRIDGE UNIVERSITY PRESS
BY
SIR ARTHUR QUILLER-COUCH
AND JOHN DOVER WILSON

AS YOU LIKE IT

AS YOU LIKE IT

CAMBRIDGE UNIVERSITY PRESS

Published by the Syndics of the Cambridge University Press
Bentley House, 200 Euston Road, London, NW1 2DB
American Branch: 32 East 57th Street, New York, N.Y. 10022

ISBNS:
0 521 07527 0 hard covers
0 521 09470 4 paperback

First published 1926
Reprinted 1948
Reprinted as Pocket edition (with corrections) 1957
Reprinted as first edition 1959 1965
First paperback edition 1968
Reprinted 1971 1973

First printed in Great Britain at the University Press, Cambridge
Reprinted in Great Britain by Hazell Watson & Viney Ltd,
Aylesbury, Bucks

CONTENTS

AS YOU LIKE IT

I

In *As You Like It*—the very title is auspicious—an Editor may take holiday and, after winning through Quarto thicket after thicket obedient to the Folio order, feel that he has earned a right to expatiate, enjoy his while in Arden and fleet the time carelessly. For no Quarto of the copy, entered provisionally by Master Roberts in the Stationers' Register and 'stayed,' whatever the reason of the staying, is extant if it ever existed. Our only text is that of the First Folio of 1623, to be considered with a few futile, mostly perfunctory, alterations in the later Folios, and more seriously with a few conjectured emendations by editors who in handling the text of this play have here and there been happy and once or twice convincing. But all this is dealt with in our *Note on the Copy* and lies apart from our present business.

II

Just as fortunately, from an Editor's point of view, we have no need to trouble our heads over 'sources.' *As You Like It* plainly derives almost all the plot it has from a novel by Thomas Lodge, *Euphues' Golden Legacie*, first published in 1590. Lodge derived a part of his story and of its *mise-en-scène* from *The Coke's Tale of Gamelyn*, left in MS by Chaucer, doubtless in MS accessible to Lodge and others, but not (so far as we know) actually printed until 1720 and included in some later editions of *The Canterbury Tales*. It was never fathered by Chaucer, never meant for a *Coke's Tale*, but was probably written out by Chaucer in the rough to be told by the Yeoman.

On this we cannot do better than quote Skeat:

Some have supposed, with great reason, that this tale occurs among the rest because it is one which Chaucer intended to recast, although, in fact, he did not live to rewrite a single line of it. This is the more likely because the tale is a capital one in itself, well worthy of being rewritten even by so great a poet; indeed, it is well known that the plot of the favourite play known to us all by the title of *As You Like It* was derived from it at second-hand. But I cannot but protest against the stupidity of the botcher whose hand wrote about it, 'The Coke's Tale of Gamelyn.' This was done because it happened to be found *next after* the 'Coke's Tale.'...The fitness of things ought to show at once that this 'Tale of Gamelyn,' a tale of the woods in true Robin Hood style, could only have been placed in the mouth of him 'who bare a mighty bow,' and who knew all the ways of wood-craft; in one word, of the Yeoman....And we get hence the additional hint, that the Yeoman's Tale was to have followed the Coke's Tale, a tale of fresh country life succeeding one of the close back-streets of the city. No better place could be found for it.

The Tale of Gamelyn (as the reader may remember) runs in this fashion:

Litheth and lesteneth || and herkeneth aright,
And ye schulle heere a talking || of a doughty knight;
Sire Johan of Boundys || was his rightë name...

and he leaves three sons. The eldest, succeeding to the estate, misuses the youngest brother, who triumphs in a wrestling-bout and, escaping to the greenwood with an old retainer, Adam the Spencer, becomes an outlaw. The eldest brother, Johan, as sheriff, pursues him—just as the proud sheriff of Nottingham pursues Robin Hood. He is taken, and bailed; returns, in ballad-fashion (like the Heir of Linne, for example), just in time to save his bail, and the wicked Johan is sent to the gallows.

But Gamelyn most probably derives from a yet older ballad of Gandelyn, Robin Hood's fere in the greenwood and avenger of his death:

I herde a carpyng of a clerk,
Al at yone wodes ende,
Of gode Robyn and Gandeleyn;
Was ther non other thynge—
Robynn lyth in grene wode bowndyn.

Upon this artless balladry Lodge stitched and embroidered, in his own manner and Lyly's, a story of court love. We are not concerned to seek whether he derived this from another story or simply invented it—and it is a pretty story anyhow. We concern ourselves only with the fact that Shakespeare took it to convert it to his own use, and note with an antiquarian interest certain names that persist—Rosalind, who becomes Ganymede as in the story, Aliena (Celia) who in the novel changes her name from Alinda, and the faithful old retainer Adam, whose name persists down from *The Tale of Gamelyn*— where he is Adam the Spencer—and is the name of the character which (tradition says) Shakespeare as an actor performed in his own play.

The name of the young champion and Rosalind's lover in the novel is Rosader. Shakespeare perhaps invented 'Orlando' as opponent to his bad brother 'Oliver'—'a Roland for his Oliver.' We observe that he wears the Christian name of his father Sir Rowland de Boys with a difference, as becomes a younger son.

Let us here remark that all the fugitives reach this Forest of Arden leg-weary and almost dead-beat. Sighs Rosalind, 'O Jupiter! how weary are my spirits!' invoking Jupiter as a Ganymede should. Touchstone retorts, 'I care not for my spirits, if my legs were not weary'; and Celia entreats, 'I pray you, bear with me, I cannot go no further': as, later on, old Adam echoes, 'Dear master, I can go no further'; and again, we remember, Oliver arrives footsore, in rags, and stretches himself to sleep, so dog-tired that even a snake, coiling about his throat, fails to awaken him. It is only the young athlete Orlando who bears the journey well.

III

But a word or two must be said on the change which overtakes all the travellers as soon as they cross the frontier of this forest into Arden, so entirely different from Lodge's forest of Ardennes.

To begin with, we can never understand the happiest in Shakespeare, without a sense of his native wood-magic. It may be too fanciful to say that he had something of the Faun in him: but certain it is that in play after play he gets his people into a woodland, or a wooded isle, where all are ringed around with enchantment, and escape the better for it. It is so in *A Mid-summer-Night's Dream*, in *A Winter's Tale*, in *The Tempest*. Men and women are lost to the world for a time, to indulge their own happy proclivities and go back somehow regenerated. We are not surprised by anything that happens within this magic fence. Within Arden we have snakes and lionesses, as within the impossible sea-coast of Bohemia, we find the stage-direction, *Exit pursued by a bear*. Titania fondles a clown and kisses the ass's head with which Puck has decorated him. Strange hounds pursue Stephano and Trinculo. Caliban is as credible as Audrey. Above all presides the tolerant magician who, in this play, assembles Dukes and courtiers—calling fools into a circle—providing them with healthy criticism of their folly. But this is not all, or by any means all. This Arden, on the south bank of Avon, endeared to him by its very name (name of his mother), had been the haunt where he caught his first 'native wood-notes wild,' as the path by the stream had been his, known to this day as the Lovers' Walk.

Time has softened down Stoneleigh-in-Arden to a stately park, with Avon streaming through; but the deer are there yet, and the ford that 'Makes sweet music with the enamelled stones' over which the deer splash—bucks leading in single file, does following in a small cohort; and there are the gnarled oaks with antique roots twisting through the bank, mirrored in pools to which the water slides over sandstone slabs and through runnels. On the left hand, under the spread of more oaks, chestnuts, wych-elms, with vistas of woodland film and of fern over which rise antlers of the herd, and over which, with no stretch of imagination, we can still see the crooks of Phebe and Silvius moving, beribboned, decorated to a model old as Sicily. Just as easily can we see Audrey, William and Sir Oliver Martext blundering into the landscape.

To put it shortly, he who knows Arden has looked into the heart of England and heard the birds sing in the green midmost of a moated island. Herein possibly lies the reason why, of all Shakespeare's plays, *As You Like It* has never crossed the Channel, to be understood by Continent sanctioners, readers, critics. An American visitor to Europe is reported as having said that, while many sights were wonderful, two struck him dumb, so many miles were they beyond promise or expectancy. The first the array of Velasquez canvases at Madrid; the second, the exuberant, almost violent rush of leaf, song, green beauty in our May-time. To men of Shakespeare's generation, after winter's necessary hardship, the transformation, the miracle, must have been yet more surprising. But we at any rate have known it, and our point is here that continental critics who have not seen the phenomenon or heard the birds singing through it, cannot understand this particular play. They have their own spring-tide, and following seasons: but not just *this*. The Germans especially are like the Wise Men of Gotham, 'all at sea in a bowl.' They are sailing, in a bowl, on perilous seas of which they possess no chart. Fortunately for the mirth of Shakespeare's countrymen they now and again cancel each other out. Let us set the solemn Ulrici and the solemn Gervinus side by side.

ULRICI.

The general comic view of life is reflected throughout the whole play, and forms the foundation and platform upon which the action moves.... The motives which set the whole in motion are merely chance, the unintentional encounter of persons and incidents, and the freaks, caprices and humours, the sentiments, feelings and emotions, to which the various personages recklessly give way in what they do and leave undone. Nowhere does the representation treat of conscious plans, definite resolves, decided aims and objects; nowhere do we find preconsidered or, in fact, deeper, motives proceeding from the inmost nature of the characters. The characters themselves, even though clearly and correctly delineated, are generally drawn in light, hurried outlines, but are full of life, gay and bold in action, and quick in decision; they appear, as already said, either inconstant, variable, going from one extreme to the other, or possess such a vast amount of imagination, sensitiveness, and love for what is romantic and adventurous that their conduct, to a prosaic mind, can only appear thoughtless, capricious and arbitrary; and such a mind would be inclined to call them all fools, oddities, and fantastic creatures.

GERVINUS.

The sweetest salve in misery, so runs 'the golden legacy' of the Novel, is patience, and the only medicine for want is contentment. Misfortune is to be defied with equanimity, and our lot be met with resignation. Hence, both the women and Orlando mock at Fortune, and disregard her power. All the three principal figures (or, including Oliver, four) have this fate in common, that to all their external misfortunes, to banishment and to poverty, there is added a new evil (for so it is regarded) love. Even this they strive to encounter with the same weapons, with control and with moderation, not yielding too much, not seeking too much, with more regard to virtue and nature than to wealth and position, just as Rosalind chooses the inferior (*nachgeborene*) Orlando, and just as Oliver chooses the shepherdess Celia. It is in reference to this that the pair of pastoral lovers are brought into contrast; Silvius loves too ardently, while Phebe loves too prudishly. If this moral reflection be expressed in a word, it is Self-control, Equanimity, Serenity in outward sorrow and inward suffering, whereof we here may learn the price. That this thought lies at the core of Shakespeare's comedy is scarcely at the first glance conceivable, so wholly is every reflection eliminated, so completely is there, in the lightest and freest play of the action and the dialogue, merely a picture sketched out before us.

On this we simply remark that absurdly as these two critics contradict one another, neither is right and each is equally wrong, because neither one nor the other has a notion what he is talking about.

Gervinus' and Ulrici's nescience of English woodland may be forgiven. But their dealing thus with Arden *in impari materia* strikes us as less excusable when we reflect that Shakespeare—who exiles a French Duke and courtiers upon the banks of Avon just as nonchalantly as in *A Midsummer-Night's Dream* he peopled an Athenian wood with Warwickshire fairies—has been at pains to provide us with a couple of his own moralists and philosophisers upon the passing show. Are we, on the face of it, likely to do as well with Gervinus and Ulrici as with Jaques and Touchstone?

IV

Let us consider Shakespeare's own pair of critics briefly and in their quiddity. Jaques has followed the exiled Duke to the forest and for what reason no one knows: in loyalty, likely enough: but if in loyalty (as many a sardonic man will go any distance for it, yet conceal devotion as a proud personal secret) he will carry no hint of this on his sleeve. He is the professed cynical moralist and something of an egoist too, with a conscious pose. He discerns the exiled Duke's talk and Amiens' song about the salutary effect of the winter wind (which by the way does not blow at all in the story) to be humbug, and in his fashion with his *Ducdame,* goes some way to expose it. But he consents with the folly in its practice. He is courtier as well as moraliser and has been (we gather) an easy liver in his time and has come through it, like many another easy liver (say Solomon himself), with a certain addiction of proverbs to the tongue—polite ones, to be sure; but, partly it may be, because they hold this reserve of politeness, concealing himself beneath apparent outspokenness and railing, he misses as a critic to be quite effective. The polite French hardly realise this: they incline to consider him the central figure of the stage—and George Sand married him, in her version, to Celia! One can better imagine Shakespeare marrying him to an arrant shrew, or even giving him a belated capture of the wench Audrey from Touchstone who yields her on some ridiculous, extravagant point of punctilio.

But on quite another score, this figure of Jaques, the melancholy, the contemplative—never getting to action beyond declamation and moralising—must give food for thought to any student of Shakespeare. He upon a fanciful comedy intrudes a figure, brooding on the ways of humankind, draped (we all visualise Jaques to be so draped) in a careful cloak of black. As yet he forwards no action, stands outside, plays no part save that of observer, amused critic: and in this comedy of ours he becomes a 'convertite' and hangs up his subtle cloak in a cell, we having no further dramatic use for him. But this contemplative man in his 'inky cloak' persists in Shakespeare's mind to be oppressed by dreadful responsibility, to be forced into action by most tragic pressure of fate. It happens so: it persists to most tragic violence: but allowing for this circumstantial pressure, let us compare Jaques with Hamlet and his—

What a piece of work is a man, etc.

V

Touchstone is, of course, a deliberately opposed commentator; but still a commentator, and a deal nearer to earth and her genuine well-springs than our philosophic Jaques. Those who see the characters in this Arden in terms of colour beneath the green boughs, will not miss to contrast Touchstone's motley with Jaques' dark habit: to see him, for instance, turning himself on the stage against Arden's background as he answers Corin's question, 'And how like you this shepherd's life, Master Touchstone?'

Truly, shepherd, in respect of itself, it is a good life [*Here turning so that one side of him itself presents green upon green*]; but in respect that it is a shepherd's life, it is naught [*Here opposing the scarlet side, and so on throughout the speech*].

The virtues we must stress are Touchstone's loyalty and complete honesty. For the loyalty, he follows to the forest with just so much unquestioning unsolicited loyalty as the Fool in *King Lear* shows to his lord and master. It seems to us, examined, almost as beautiful, and it gets almost as little thanks. But it has, with one as with the other, performed its service. And in *As You Like It* as in *Lear* this part of the Fool is to help insanity or sentimentality back to sense: to be the 'touch-stone,' the test of normal, all the more effective for being presented in jest, under motley. 'Lord! what fools these mortals be!' Our Touchstone, transformed from a 'roynish clown' into a mundane philosopher from the moment he reaches the forest, knows what he knows and why he must mate with Audrey. He gives us his reasons none too delicately: but we have proved his character, his tenacity in faith, and his grossest reasons (they are not so gross, after all) help marvellously to un-sentimentalise a play which might easily have lost itself in sentiment, to recall its waywardness, to give it to us for the thing it is, so bewitching and yet so forthright, so honest, so salutary.

VI

In the faithful love of Celia for Rosalind (we think) it has not been noted, or not sufficiently noted, that Shakespeare had, for his age, a curiously deep understanding of sisterly love and loyalty to troth. Troth between two men-friends was accepted as a convention, almost: for his friend a man would sacrifice wife, mistress and children: and maybe in our Introduction to *The Two Gentlemen of Verona* we did not allow enough for this in our comments upon Valentine's amazing offer to Proteus:

> All that was mine in Silvia I give thee.

That, however, reaches to the limit of the medieval male convention. One finds little trace before Shakespeare of that *sisterly* devotion into which he has already given us sweet insight in *A Midsummer-Night's Dream* (not to dwell on Beatrice's valiancy for injured Hero and her risk of a man's love on the challenge 'Kill Claudio'). Let us listen to Helena reproaching Hermia:

> We, Hermia, like two artificial gods,
> Have with our needles created both one flower,
> Both on one sampler, sitting on one cushion,
> Both warbling of one song, both in one key;
> As if our hands, our sides, voices, and minds,
> Had been incorporate. So we grew together,
> Like to a double cherry, seeming parted;
> But yet an union in partition...

But love for man parts this double 'cherry,' as it so often does. In *As You Like It* Celia, the provident, throughout follows Rosalind, giving up father, state and fortune in steady fidelity.

Rosalind is after her lover; and plays the action through with prettiest trickery and witchery. But is Orlando really tricked to the end? He may pin foolish ballads on trees where (as in *Love's Labour's Lost*) nobody concerned is likely to read 'em. But can anyone read the later scenes of this play and believe that he had not at any rate a shrewd suspicion that this Ganymede was his Rosalind: or even that the exiled Duke himself had not some inkling?

> I do remember in this shepherd-boy
> Some lively touches of my daughter's favour.

No: we are in Arden, where all is deception, but there is no deception save self-deception, and even that very pretty, and pardonable. At any time, in any clearing, two page-boys may wander in and sing a carol of a lover and his lass. As another carol of the time has it:

> Hey, nonny no!
> Men are fools who wish to die!
> Is't not fine to dance and sing
> When the bells of death do ring?
> Is't not fine to swim in wine,
> And turn upon the toe,
> And sing hey, nonny no!
> When the winds blow
> And the seas flow?
> Hey, nonny no!

It is all charming make-believe in this play, with Jaques and Touchstone as correctives or sedatives. To philosophise it is as absurd as to sit down and count out its impossibilities of time, 'duration of action,' geography, fauna. But the heart of it is as sound as the heart of an Idyll of Theocritus or an Eclogue of Virgil. You may call it artificial: you may prove, for instance, that the chiming quartet, 'And so am I for Phebe,' 'And I for Ganymede,' 'And I for Rosalind,' 'And I for no woman,' etc. is artificial. But its pastoral guise is the guise of a feeling that goes deeper into mortal concern than criticism can easily penetrate.

VII

What shall we say of the ending and its hymeneals? The ending is huddled up, of course: any Elizabethan playwright took that way, and the plays of Shakespeare, labelled Comedy, History, or Tragedy, take it again and again. Yet even after a lion and a snake, these classical nuptials seem wildly incongruous with the English Arden Shakespeare has evolved for us out of his young memories. It may very well be that, as our texts reach us, they were adapted out of Christian to Pagan ceremonial in obedience to royal wish or statute. But it matters nothing, surely. The gods change, but literature persists: and if the *deus Terminus* of our woodland be the altar of Hymen, who shall gainsay? Surely no one who has known Catullus.

It is all just as believable as that Oliver has changed heart by converse with a friar casually met, or Jaques hung up his cloak in a house of convertites. Arden, having room for all fancy beneath its oaks, has room for all reconciliations on its fringe, and Hymen, surely, makes a better sealer of vows than, say, Martext, discoverable in that land. For after all, every passenger goes through it under enchantment, and as in *The Tempest* Ferdinand and Miranda prepare their wedlock through sweet Pagan rites—as in *The Tempest* all are held under spell—so all step clear of the forest, as of the Isle, to common life, restored to it through nuptial mirth not of the Church—of the Golden Age, rather. We are recalled to normal life because Shakespeare is, at the end, of all men the most commonsensical. We win out of Arden, or a rainbowed island, to end our days as a burgess, proprietor of respectable New Place. But in youth—and it is observable how almost all great authors draw throughout life upon their youth, bringing forth treasures both new and old—in our author's house are many mansions, and we have loitered through Arden, courted under the boughs, laughed, loved, housed in the wilderness, listened to Avon and heard the song.

Q.

TO THE READER

The following is a brief description of the punctuation and other typographical devices employed in the text, which have been more fully explained in the *Note on Punctuation* and the *Textual Introduction* to be found in *The Tempest* volume:

An obelisk (†) implies corruption or emendation, and suggests a reference to the Notes.

A single bracket at the beginning of a speech signifies an 'aside.'

Four dots represent a *full-stop* in the original, except when it occurs at the end of a speech, and they mark a long pause. Original *colons* or *semicolons*, which denote a somewhat shorter pause, are retained, or represented as three dots when they appear to possess special dramatic significance. Similarly, significant *commas* have been given as dashes.

Round brackets are taken from the original, and mark a significant change of voice; when the original brackets seem to imply little more than the drop in tone accompanying parenthesis, they are conveyed by commas or dashes.

In plays for which both Folio and Quarto texts exist, passages taken from the text not selected as the basis for the present edition will be enclosed within square brackets. Lines which Shakespeare apparently intended to cancel, have been marked off by frame-brackets.

Single inverted commas (' ') are editorial; double ones (" ") derive from the original, where they are used to draw attention to maxims, quotations, etc.

The reference number for the first line is given at the head of each page. Numerals in square brackets are placed at the beginning of the traditional acts and scenes.

The scene: Oliver's house, Duke Frederick's court, and the Forest of Arden

CHARACTERS IN THE PLAY

A banished DUKE

FREDERICK, *his brother, and usurper of his dominions*

AMIENS
JAQUES } *lords attending on the banished Duke*

LE BEAU, *a courtier attending upon Frederick*

CHARLES, *wrestler to Frederick*

OLIVER
JAQUES } *sons of Sir Rowland de Boys*
ORLANDO

ADAM
DENNIS } *servants to Oliver*

TOUCHSTONE, *a clown*

SIR OLIVER MARTEXT, *a vicar*

CORIN
SILVIUS } *shepherds*

WILLIAM, *a country fellow, in love with Audrey*

A person representing Hymen

ROSALIND, *daughter to the banished Duke*

CELIA, *daughter to Frederick*

PHEBE, *a shepherdess*

AUDREY, *a country wench*

Lords, pages, foresters, and attendants

AS YOU LIKE IT

AS YOU LIKE IT

An orchard, near Oliver's house

ORLANDO and ADAM

Orlando. As I remember, Adam, it was upon this fashion:† a' bequeathed me by will but poor thousand crowns and, as thou say'st, charged my brother on his blessing to breed me well: and there begins my sadness...My brother Jaques he keeps at school, and report speaks goldenly of his profit: for my part, he keeps me rustically at home, or, to speak more properly, stays me here at home unkept: for call you that 'keeping' for a gentleman of my birth, that differs not from the stalling of an ox? His horses are bred better—for, besides that 10 they are fair with their feeding, they are taught their manage, and to that end riders dearly hired: but I, his brother, gain nothing under him but growth, for the which his animals on his dunghills are as much bound to him as I...Besides this nothing that he so plentifully gives me, the something that nature gave me his countenance seems to take from me: he lets me feed with his hinds, bars me the place of a brother, and, as much as in him lies, mines my gentility with my education.... This is it, Adam, that grieves me—and the spirit of my 20 father, which I think is within me, begins to mutiny against this servitude....I will no longer endure it, though yet I know no wise remedy how to avoid it.

OLIVER enters the orchard

Adam. Yonder comes my master, your brother.

Orlando. Go apart, Adam, and thou shalt hear how he will shake me up. [*Adam withdraws a little*

Oliver. Now, sir! what make you here?

Orlando. Nothing: I am not taught to make any thing.

Oliver. What mar you then, sir?

30 *Orlando.* Marry, sir, I am helping you to mar that which God made, a poor unworthy brother of yours, with idleness.

Oliver. Marry, sir, be better employed, and be naught awhile.

Orlando. Shall I keep your hogs and eat husks with them? What prodigal portion have I spent, that I should come to such penury?

Oliver. Know you where you are, sir?

Orlando. O, sir, very well: here in your orchard.

40 *Oliver.* Know you before whom, sir?

Orlando. Ay, better than him I am before knows me... I know you are my eldest brother, and in the gentle condition of blood you should so know me...The courtesy of nations allows you my better, in that you are the first-born, but the same tradition takes not away my blood, were there twenty brothers betwixt us: I have as much of my father in me as you, albeit I confess your coming before me is nearer to his reverence.

Oliver. What, boy!   [*he strikes him*

50 *Orlando.* Come, come, elder brother, you are too young in this.   [*he takes him by the throat*

Oliver. Wilt thou lay hands on me, villain?

Orlando. I am no villain: I am the youngest son of Sir Rowland de Boys, he was my father, and he is thrice a villain that says such a father begot villains...Wert thou not my brother, I would not take this hand from thy throat, till this other had pulled out thy tongue for saying so—thou hast railed on thyself.   [*Adam comes forward*

Adam. Sweet masters, be patient. For your father's
60 remembrance, be at accord.

neither, than with safety of a pure blush thou mayst in honour come off again.

Rosalind. What shall be our sport then?

Celia. Let us sit and mock the good housewife Fortune from her wheel, that her gifts may henceforth be bestowed equally.

Rosalind. I would we could do so; for her benefits are mightily misplaced, and the bountiful blind woman doth most mistake in her gifts to women.

Celia. 'Tis true, for those that she makes fair she scarce makes honest, and those that she makes honest she makes very ill-favouredly.

Rosalind. Nay, now thou goest from Fortune's office to Nature's: Fortune reigns in gifts of the world, not in the lineaments of Nature.

Touchstone approaches

Celia. No? When Nature hath made a fair creature, may she not by Fortune fall into the fire? Though Nature hath given us wit to flout at Fortune, hath not Fortune sent in this fool to cut off the argument?

Rosalind. Indeed, there is Fortune too hard for Nature, when Fortune makes Nature's natural the cutter-off of Nature's wit.

Celia. Peradventure this is not Fortune's work neither, but Nature's, who perceiveth our natural wits too dull to reason of such goddesses and hath sent this natural for our whetstone: for always the dulness of the fool is the whetstone of the wits....How now, wit! whither wander you?

Touchstone. Mistress, you must come away to your father.

Celia. Were you made the messenger?

Touchstone. No, by mine honour, but I was bid to come for you.

Rosalind. Where learned you that oath, fool?

Touchstone. Of a certain knight, that swore by his
60 honour they were good pancakes, and swore by his
honour the mustard was naught: now I'll stand to it,
the pancakes were naught and the mustard was good,
and yet was not the knight forsworn.

Celia. How prove you that, in the great heap of your
knowledge?

Rosalind. Ay, marry, now unmuzzle your wisdom.

Touchstone. Stand you both forth now: stroke your
chins, and swear by your beards that I am a knave.

Celia. By our beards (if we had them) thou art.

70 *Touchstone.* By my knavery (if I had it) then I were:
but if you swear by that that is not, you are not forsworn:
no more was this knight, swearing by his honour, for he
never had any; or if he had, he had sworn it away,
before ever he saw those pancakes or that mustard.

Celia. Prithee, who is't that thou mean'st?

Touchstone [*to Rosalind*]. One that old †Frederick,
your father, loves.

Rosalind. My father's love is enough to honour him.
Enough! speak no more of him—you'll be whipped for
80 taxation one of these days.

Touchstone. The more pity, that fools may not speak
wisely what wise men do foolishly.

Celia. By my troth, thou sayest true: for since the little
wit that fools have was silenced, the little foolery that
wise men have makes a great show...Here comes
Monsieur Le Beau.

LE BEAU is seen hurrying towards them

Rosalind. With his mouth full of news.

Celia. Which he will put on us, as pigeons feed their
young.

Rosalind. Then shall we be news-crammed.   90

Celia. All the better: we shall be the more marketable.
Bon jour, Monsieur Le Beau! what's the news?

Le Beau. Fair princess, you have lost much good sport.

Celia. Sport? Of what colour?

Le Beau. What colour, madam? How shall I answer
you?

Rosalind. As wit and fortune will.

Touchstone [*mocking him*]. Or as the Destinies decree.

Celia. Well said, that was laid on with a trowel.

Touchstone. Nay, if I keep not my rank—   100

Rosalind. Thou losest thy old smell.

Le Beau. You amaze me, ladies: I would have told
you of good wrestling, which you have lost the sight of.

Rosalind. Yet tell us the manner of the wrestling.

Le Beau. I will tell you the beginning, and, if it please
your ladyships, you may see the end—for the best is yet
to do, and here, where you are, they are coming to
perform it.

Celia. Well, the beginning, that is dead and buried?

Le Beau. There comes an old man and his three sons—   110

Celia. I could match this beginning with an old tale.

Le Beau. Three proper young men, of excellent growth
and presence.

Rosalind. With bills on their necks: 'Be it known unto
all men by these presents.'

Le Beau. The eldest of the three wrestled with Charles,
the duke's wrestler, which Charles in a moment threw
him and broke three of his ribs, that there is little hope
of life in him: so he served the second, and so the third...
Yonder they lie, the poor old man their father making 120
such pitiful dole over them that all the beholders take
his part with weeping.

Rosalind. Alas!

Touchstone. But what is the sport, monsieur, that the ladies have lost?

Le Beau. Why, this that I speak of.

Touchstone. Thus men may grow wiser every day. It is the first time that ever I heard breaking of ribs was sport for ladies.

130   *Celia.* Or I, I promise thee.

Rosalind. But is there any else longs to see this broken music in his sides? is there yet another dotes upon rib-breaking? Shall we see this wrestling, cousin?

Le Beau. You must if you stay here, for here is the place appointed for the wrestling, and they are ready to perform it.

Celia. Yonder, sure, they are coming....Let us now stay and see it.

A flourish of trumpets. Duke FREDERICK *with his lords,* ORLANDO, CHARLES, *and attendants cross the lawn towards a plot prepared for the wrestling*

Duke Frederick. Come on. Since the youth will not 140   be entreated, his own peril on his forwardness.

Rosalind. Is yonder the man?

Le Beau. Even he, madam.

Celia. Alas, he is too young: yet he looks successfully.

Duke Frederick. How now, daughter and cousin! are you crept hither to see the wrestling?

Rosalind. Ay, my liege, so please you give us leave.

Duke Frederick. You will take little delight in it, I can tell you, there is such odds in the man...In pity of the challenger's youth I would fain dissuade him, but he 150   will not be entreated....Speak to him, ladies—see if you can move him.

Celia. Call him hither, good Monsieur Le Beau.

Duke Frederick. Do so: I'll not be by. [*he takes his seat*

Le Beau. Monsieur the challenger, the princess calls for you.

Orlando [*comes forward*]. I attend them with all respect and duty.

Rosalind. Young man, have you challenged Charles the wrestler?

Orlando [*bows*]. No, fair princess: he is the general 160 challenger. I come but in, as others do, to try with him the strength of my youth.

Celia. Young gentleman, your spirits are too bold for your years...You have seen cruel proof of this man's strength. If you saw yourself with your eyes, or knew yourself with your judgement, the fear of your adventure would counsel you to a more equal enterprise.... We pray you, for your own sake, to embrace your own safety, and give over this attempt.

Rosalind. Do, young sir, your reputation shall not 170 therefore be misprized: we will make it our suit to the duke that the wrestling might not go forward.

Orlando. I beseech you, punish me not with your hard thoughts, wherein I confess me much guilty to deny so fair and excellent ladies any thing. But let your fair eyes and gentle wishes go with me to my trial: wherein if I be foiled, there is but one shamed that was never gracious; if killed, but one dead that is willing to be so: I shall do my friends no wrong, for I have none to lament me; the world no injury, for in it I have nothing: 180 only in the world I fill up a place, which may be better supplied when I have made it empty.

Rosalind. The little strength that I have, I would it were with you.

Celia. And mine, to eke out hers.

Rosalind. Fare you well...Pray heaven, I be deceived in you!

Celia. Your heart's desires be with you!

Charles [*calls*]. Come, where is this young gallant that
190 is so desirous to lie with his mother earth?

Orlando. Ready, sir, but his will hath in it a more
modest working.

Duke Frederick. You shall try but one fall.

Charles. No, I warrant your grace, you shall not entreat him to a second, that have so mightily persuaded
him from a first.

Orlando. An you mean to mock me after, you should
not have mocked me before: but come your ways.

Rosalind. Now, Hercules be thy speed, young man!
200 *Celia.* I would I were invisible, to catch the strong
fellow by the leg.

> [*The wrestling begins: they close, Orlando
> skilfully securing the better hold*

Rosalind. O excellent young man!

Celia. If I had a thunderbolt in mine eye, I can tell
who should down.

[*The wrestlers sway and strain to and fro, till of a sudden
Charles is thrown heavily to the ground; a great shout*

Duke Frederick [*rises*]. No more, no more.

Orlando. Yes, I beseech your grace—I am not yet well
breathed.

Duke Frederick. How dost thou, Charles?

Le Beau.   He cannot speak, my lord.

Duke Frederick. Bear him away...

> [*they take up Charles and carry him forth*
> What is thy name, young man?

210 *Orlando.* Orlando, my liege; the youngest son of Sir
Rowland de Boys.

Duke Frederick. I would thou hadst been son to some
man else.

The world esteemed thy father honourable,

But I did find him still mine enemy:
Thou shouldst have better pleased me with this deed,
Hadst thou descended from another house:
But fare thee well, thou art a gallant youth.
I would thou hadst told me of another father.
    [*Duke Frederick, Le Beau and the other lords depart*
    Celia. Were I my father, coz, would I do this?
    Orlando. I am more proud to be Sir Rowland's son,   220
His youngest son, and would not change that calling,
To be adopted heir to Frederick.
    Rosalind. My father loved Sir Rowland as his soul,
And all the world was of my father's mind.
Had I before known this young man his son,
I should have given him tears unto entreaties,
Ere he should thus have ventured.
    Celia.   Gentle cousin,
Let us go thank him, and encourage him:
My father's rough and envious disposition
Sticks me at heart...[*they rise and accost Orlando*] Sir,
        you have well deserved.   230
If you do keep your promises in love
But justly as you have exceeded promise,
Your mistress shall be happy.
    Rosalind [*takes a chain from her neck*] Gentleman,
Wear this for me...one out of suits with fortune,
That could give more, but that her hand lacks means....
Shall we go, coz?   [*she turns and walks away*
    Celia [*follows*]. Ay: fare you well, fair gentleman.
    Orlando. Can I not say, 'I thank you'? My better
        parts
Are all thrown down, and that which here stands up··
Is but a quintain, a mere lifeless block.
    Rosalind. He calls us back: my pride fell with my
        fortunes—   240

I'll ask him what he would...[*she turns again*] Did you
    call, sir?
Sir, you have wrestled well and overthrown
More than your enemies.   [*they gaze upon each other*
  Celia [*plucks her sleeve*] Will you go, coz?
  Rosalind. Have with you...Fare you well.
                [*she hastens away, Celia following*
  Orlando. What passion hangs these weights upon my
    tongue?
I cannot speak to her, yet she urged conference.

Le Beau *returns*

O poor Orlando, thou art overthrown!
Or Charles, or something weaker, masters thee.
  Le Beau. Good sir, I do in friendship counsel you
250 To leave this place...Albeit you have deserved
High commendation, true applause, and love,
Yet such is now the duke's condition,
That he misconstrues all that you have done..
The duke is humorous—what he is, indeed,
More suits you to conceive than I to speak of.
  Orlando. I thank you, sir: and, pray you, tell me this,
Which of the two was daughter of the duke,
That here was at the wrestling?
  Le Beau. Neither his daughter, if we judge by manners,
260 But yet, indeed, the smaller is his daughter.
The other is daughter to the banished duke,
And here detained by her usurping uncle,
To keep his daughter company—whose loves
Are dearer than the natural bond of sisters...
But I can tell you that of late this duke
Hath ta'en displeasure 'gainst his gentle niece,
Grounded upon no other argument
But that the people praise her for her virtues,

And pity her for her good father's sake;
And, on my life, his malice 'gainst the lady   27
Will suddenly break forth...Sir, fare you well.
Hereafter, in a better world than this,
I shall desire more love and knowledge of you.

  Orlando. I rest much bounden to you: fare you well....
                                                [Le Beau goes
Thus must I from the smoke into the smother,
From tyrant duke unto a tyrant brother....
But heavenly Rosalind!   *[he departs, musing*

[1. 3.]   *A room in the palace of Duke Frederick*

ROSALIND *on a couch with her face to the wall,* CELIA
bending over her

  Celia. Why cousin, why Rosalind...Cupid have
mercy! Not a word?
  Rosalind. Not one to throw at a dog.
  Celia. No, thy words are too precious to be cast away
upon curs, throw some of them at me; come, lame me
with reasons.
  Rosalind. Then there were two cousins laid up, when
the one should be lamed with reasons, and the other
mad without any.
  Celia. But is all this for your father?   1
  Rosalind. No, some of it is for my child's father...
[*rises*] O, how full of briars is this working-day world!
  Celia. They are but burs, cousin, thrown upon thee
in holiday foolery. If we walk not in the trodden paths,
our very petticoats will catch them.
  Rosalind. I could shake them off my coat—these burs
are in my heart.
  Celia. Hem them away.

Rosalind. I would try, if I could cry 'hem' and have
20 him.

Celia. Come, come, wrestle with thy affections.

Rosalind. O, they take the part of a better wrestler
than myself.

Celia. O, a good wish upon you! you will try in time,
in despite of a fall....But turning these jests out of service, let us talk in good earnest: is it possible, on such
a sudden, you should fall into so strong a liking with old
Sir Rowland's youngest son?

Rosalind. The duke my father loved his father dearly.

30 *Celia.* Doth it therefore ensue that you should love
his son dearly? By this kind of chase, I should hate
him, for my father hated his father dearly; yet I hate
not Orlando.

Rosalind. No, faith, hate him not, for my sake.

Celia. Why should I not? doth he not deserve well?

Rosalind. Let me love him for that, and do you love
him because I do....[*the door is flung open and* DUKE
FREDERICK *enters, preceded by attendants and the lords
of his council*] Look, here comes the duke.

40 *Celia.* With his eyes full of anger.

Duke Frederick [*pausing in the doorway*]. Mistress,
            dispatch you with your safest haste
And get you from our court.

Rosalind.   Me, uncle?

Duke Frederick.   You, cousin.
Within these ten days if that thou be'st found
So near our public court as twenty miles,
Thou diest for it.

Rosalind.   I do beseech your grace,
Let me the knowledge of my fault bear with me:
If with myself I hold intelligence
Or have acquaintance with mine own desires,

If that I do not dream or be not frantic—
As I do trust I am not—then, dear uncle,   50
Never so much as in a thought unborn
Did I offend your highness.
   Duke Frederick.   Thus do all traitors!
If their purgation did consist in words,
They are as innocent as grace itself:
Let it suffice thee that I trust thee not.
   Rosalind. Yet your mistrust cannot make me a traitor:
Tell me whereon the likelihood depends.
   Duke Frederick. Thou art thy father's daughter, there's
      enough.
   Rosalind. So was I when your highness took his
      dukedom,
So was I when your highness banished him;   60
Treason is not inherited, my lord,
Or, if we did derive it from our friends,
What's that to me? my father was no traitor.
Then, good my liege, mistake me not so much
To think my poverty is treacherous.
   Celia. Dear sovereign, hear me speak.
   Duke Frederick. Ay, Celia, we stayed her for your
      sake,
Else had she with her father ranged along.
   Celia. I did not then entreat to have her stay,
It was your pleasure and your own remorse.   70
I was too young that time to value her,
But now I know her: if she be a traitor,
Why so am I: we still have slept together,
Rose at an instant, learned, played, eat together,
And wheresoe'er we went, like Juno's swans,
Still we went coupled and inseparable.
   Duke Frederick. She is too subtle for thee, and her
      smoothness,

Her very silence and her patience
Speak to the people, and they pity her...
80 Thou art a fool—she robs thee of thy name,
And thou wilt show more bright and seem more virtuous
When she is gone: then open not thy lips.
Firm and irrevocable is my doom
Which I have passed upon her—she is banished.

   Celia. Pronounce that sentence then on me, my liege,
I cannot live out of her company.

   Duke Frederick. You are a fool...You, niece, provide
      yourself.
If you outstay the time, upon mine honour,
And in the greatness of my word, you die.

   [*he turns and leaves the room, his lords following him*
90 *Celia.* O my poor Rosalind, whither wilt thou go?
Wilt thou change fathers? I will give thee mine...
I charge thee, be not thou more grieved than I am.

   Rosalind. I have more cause.

   Celia.   Thou hast not, cousin.
Prithee, be cheerful; know'st thou not, the duke
Hath banished me his daughter?

   Rosalind.   That he hath not.

   Celia. No, hath not? Rosalind lacks then the love
Which teacheth thee that thou and I am one.
Shall we be sundred? shall we part, sweet girl?
No, let my father seek another heir...
100 Therefore devise with me how we may fly,
Whither to go and what to bear with us,
And do not seek to take your change upon you,
To bear your griefs yourself and leave me out;
For, by this heaven, now at our sorrows pale,
Say what thou canst, I'll go along with thee.

   Rosalind. Why, whither shall we go?

   Celia. To seek my uncle in the forest of Arden.

Rosalind. Alas, what danger will it be to us,
Maids as we are, to travel forth so far!
Beauty provoketh thieves sooner than gold.   110

 Celia. I'll put myself in poor and mean attire,
And with a kind of umber smirch my face,
The like do you, so shall we pass along
And never stir assailants.

 Rosalind.   Were it not better,
Because that I am more than common tall,
That I did suit me all points like a man?
A gallant curtle-axe upon my thigh,
A boar-spear in my hand, and in my heart
Lie there what hidden woman's fear there will,
We'll have a swashing and a martial outside,   120
As many other mannish cowards have
That do outface it with their semblances.

 Celia. What shall I call thee when thou art a man?

 Rosalind. I'll have no worse a name than Jove's
    own page,
And therefore look you call me Ganymede.
But what will you be called?

 Celia. Something that hath a reference to my state;
No longer Celia, but Aliena.

 Rosalind. But, cousin, what if we assayed to steal
The clownish fool out of your father's court?   130
Would he not be a comfort to our travel?

 Celia. He'll go along o'er the wide world with me,
Leave me alone to woo him...Let's away,
And get our jewels and our wealth together,
Devise the fittest time and safest way
To hide us from pursuit that will be made
After my flight...Now go we in content
To liberty, and not to banishment.   [*they go*

A.Y.L.I. – 3

[2.1.]   *The forest of Arden*

The entrance to a cave, with a spreading tree before it.
The exiled Duke, 'AMIENS and two or three Lords like
foresters' come from the cave

  Duke. Now, my co-mates and brothers in exile,
Hath not old custom made this life more sweet
Than that of painted pomp? Are not these woods
More free from peril than the envious court?
Here feel we not the penalty of Adam,
The seasons' difference?—as the icy fang
And churlish chiding of the winter's wind,
Which, when it bites and blows upon my body,
Even till I shrink with cold, I smile and say
10 'This is no flattery: these are counsellors
That feelingly persuade me what I am'...
Sweet are the uses of adversity,
Which like the toad, ugly and venomous,
Wears yet a precious jewel in his head:
And this our life, exempt from public haunt,
Finds tongues in trees, books in the running brooks,
Sermons in stones, and good in every thing.
I would not change it.
  Amiens.   Happy is your grace,
That can translate the stubbornness of fortune
20 Into so quiet and so sweet a style.
  Duke. Come, shall we go and kill us venison?
And yet it irks me the poor dappled fools,
Being native burghers of this desert city,
Should in their own confines with forkéd heads
Have their round haunches gored.
  First Lord.   Indeed, my lord,
The melancholy Jaques grieves at that,
And, in that kind, swears you do more usurp

Than doth your brother that hath banished you:
To-day my Lord of Amiens and myself
Did steal behind him as he lay along   30
Under an oak, whose antique root peeps out
Upon the brook that brawls along this wood,
To the which place a poor sequestred stag,
That from the hunter's aim had ta'en a hurt,
Did come to languish; and, indeed, my lord,
The wretched animal heaved forth such groans,
That their discharge did stretch his leathern coat
Almost to bursting, and the big round tears
Coursed one another down his innocent nose
In piteous chase: and thus the hairy fool,   40
Much markéd of the melancholy Jaques,
Stood on th'extremest verge of the swift brook,
Augmenting it with tears.
  Duke.   But what said Jaques?
Did he not moralize this spectacle?
  First Lord. O, yes, into a thousand similes.
First, for his weeping in the needless stream;
'Poor deer,' quoth he, 'thou mak'st a testament
As worldlings do, giving thy sum of more
To that which had too much': then, being there alone,
Left and abandoned of his velvet friends;   50
''Tis right,' quoth he, 'thus misery doth part
The flux of company': anon a careless herd,
Full of the pasture, jumps along by him
And never stays to greet him; 'Ay,' quoth Jaques,
'Sweep on, you fat and greasy citizens!
'Tis just the fashion; wherefore do you look
Upon that poor and broken bankrupt there?'
Thus most invectively he pierceth through
The body of the country, city, court,
Yea, and of this our life, swearing that we   60

Are mere usurpers, tyrants and what's worse,
To fright the animals and to kill them up
In their assigned and native dwelling-place.
　Duke. And did you leave him in this contemplation?
　Second Lord. We did, my lord, weeping and
　　　commenting
Upon the sobbing deer.
　Duke.　　　　　　　　Show me the place,
I love to cope him in these sullen fits,
For then he's full of matter.
　First Lord. I'll bring you to him straight.　　[*they go*

[2.2.]　*A room in the palace of Duke Frederick*

Duke FREDERICK, *lords, and attendants*

Duke Frederick. Can it be possible that no man
　　　saw them?
It cannot be. Some villains of my court
Are of consent and sufferance in this.
　First Lord. I cannot hear of any that did see her.
The ladies, her attendants of her chamber,
Saw her abed, and in the morning early
They found the bed untreasured of their mistress.
　Second Lord. My lord, the roynish clown, at whom
　　　so oft
Your grace was wont to laugh, is also missing.
10 Hisperia, the princess' gentlewoman,
Confesses that she secretly o'erheard
Your daughter and her cousin much commend
The parts and graces of the wrestler
That did but lately foil the sinewy Charles,
And she believes wherever they are gone
That youth is surely in their company.

Duke Frederick. Send to his brother, fetch that
    gallant hither.
If he be absent, bring his brother to me—
I'll make him find him: do this suddenly;
And let not search and inquisition quail   20
To bring again these foolish runaways.   *[they go*

[2. 3.]   *The orchard near Oliver's house*
       ORLANDO *and* ADAM, *meeting*

Orlando. Who's there?
   Adam. What! my young master? O my gentle master,
O my sweet master, O you memory
Of old Sir Rowland...why, what make you here?
Why are you virtuous? Why do people love you?
And wherefore are you gentle, strong, and valiant?
Why would you be so fond to overcome
The bonny prizer of the humorous duke?
Your praise is come too swiftly home before you.
Know you not, master, to some kind of men   10
Their graces serve them but as enemies?
No more do yours; your virtues, gentle master,
Are sanctified and holy traitors to you...
O, what a world is this, when what is comely
Envenoms him that bears it!
   Orlando. Why, what's the matter?
   Adam.   O unhappy youth,
Come not within these doors; within this roof
The enemy of all your graces lives...
Your brother—no, no brother—yet the son
(Yet not the son, I will not call him son)   20
Of him I was about to call his father—
Hath heard your praises, and this night he means
To burn the lodging where you use to lie,
And you within it: if he fail of that,

He will have other means to cut you off:
I overheard him...and his practices...
This is no place, this house is but.a butchery;
Abhor it, fear it, do not enter it.

   Orlando. Why, whither, Adam, wouldst thou have
     me go?

30   *Adam*. No matter whither, so you come not here.

   Orlando. What, wouldst thou have me go and beg
     my food?
Or with a base and boisterous sword enforce
A thievish living on the common road?
This I must do, or know not what to do:
Yet this I will not do, do how I can—
I rather will subject me to the malice
Of a diverted blood and bloody brother.

   Adam. But do not so: I have five hundred crowns,
The thrifty hire I saved under your father,

40 Which I did store to be my foster-nurse
When service should in my old limbs lie lame,
And unregarded age in corners thrown.
Take that, and He that doth the ravens feed,
Yea providently caters for the sparrow,
Be comfort to my age...[*he gives him a bag*] Here is
     the gold;
All this I give you. Let me be your servant.
Though I look old, yet I am strong and lusty;
For in my youth I never did apply
Hot and rebellious liquors in my blood,

50 Nor did not with unbashful forehead woo
The means of weakness and debility.
Therefore my age is as a lusty winter,
Frosty, but kindly: let me go with you,
I'll do the service of a younger man
In all your business and necessities.

Orlando. O good old man, how well in thee appears
The constant service of the antique world,
When service sweat for duty, not for meed!
Thou art not for the fashion of these times,
Where none will sweat but for promotion,　　60
And having that do choke their service up
Even with the having—it is not so with thee...
But, poor old man, thou prun'st a rotten tree,
That cannot so much as a blossom yield,
In lieu of all thy pains and husbandry.
But come thy ways, we'll go along together,
And ere we have thy youthful wages spent,
We'll light upon some settled low content.
　Adam. Master, go on, and I will follow thee
To the last gasp with truth and loyalty.　　70
From seventeen years till now almost fourscore
Here lived I, but now live here no more.
At seventeen years many their fortunes seek,
But at fourscore it is too late a week.
Yet fortune cannot recompense me better
Than to die well, and not my master's debtor.
　　　　　　　　　　[they leave the orchard

[2. 4.]　*A clearing in the outskirts of the forest*

Rosalind (*as* Ganymede) *clad as a boy in forester's
dress, and* Celia (*as* Aliena) *clad as a shepherdess,
together with* Touchstone, *approach slowly and fling
themselves upon the ground under a tree*

　Rosalind. O Jupiter! how weary are my spirits!
　Touchstone. I care not for my spirits, if my legs were
not weary.

　Rosalind. I could find in my heart to disgrace my
man's apparel, and to cry like a woman: but I must

comfort the weaker vessel, as doublet-and-hose ought to show itself courageous to petticoat: therefore courage, good Aliena!

Celia. I pray you, bear with me, I cannot go no
10 further.

Touchstone. For my part, I had rather bear with you than bear you: yet I should bear no cross if I did bear you, for I think you have no money in your purse.

Rosalind. Well, this is the forest of Arden!

Touchstone. Ay, now am I in Arden, the more fool I. When I was at home I was in a better place, but travellers must be content.

Rosalind. Ay,
Be so, good Touchstone...

    CORIN *and* SILVIUS *draw near*

        Look you, who comes here—
20 A young man and an old in solemn talk.

Corin. That is the way to make her scorn you still.

Silvius. O Corin, that thou knew'st how I do love her!

Corin. I partly guess: for I have loved ere now.

Silvius. No, Corin, being old, thou canst not guess,
Though in thy youth thou wast as true a lover
As ever sighed upon a midnight pillow:
But if thy love were ever like to mine—
As sure I think did never man love so—
How many actions most ridiculous
30 Hast thou been drawn to by thy fantasy?

Corin. Into a thousand that I have forgotten.

Silvius. O, thou didst then ne'er love so heartily.
If thou rememberest not the slightest folly
That ever love did make thee run into,
Thou hast not loved....
Or if thou hast not sat as I do now,
Wearing thy hearer in thy mistress' praise,

Thou hast not loved....
Or if thou hast not broke from company
Abruptly, as my passion now makes me,   40
Thou hast not loved....
O Phebe, Phebe, Phebe!
   [*he buries his face in his hands and runs into the forest*
   Rosalind. Alas, poor shepherd! searching of thy wound,
I have by hard adventure found mine own.

Touchstone. And I mine: I remember, when I was in
love I broke my sword upon a stone, and bid him take
that for coming a-night to Jane Smile, and I remember
the kissing of her batler and the cow's dugs that her
pretty chopt hands had milked; and I remember the
wooing of a peascod instead of her, from whom I took   50
two cods, and giving her them again, said with weeping
tears, 'Wear these for my sake'...We that are true lovers
run into strange capers; but as all is mortal in nature,
so is all nature in love mortal in folly.

Rosalind. Thou speak'st wiser than thou art ware of.

Touchstone. Nay, I shall ne'er be ware of mine own
wit till I break my shins against it.

Rosalind. Jove, Jove! this shepherd's passion
        Is much upon my fashion.

Touchstone. And mine—but it grows something stale   60
with me.

Celia. I pray you, one of you question yond man
If he for gold will give us any food,
I faint almost to death.

Touchstone.   Holla; you, clown!

Rosalind. Peace, fool, he's not thy kinsman.

Corin.   Who calls?

Touchstone. Your betters, sir.

Corin.   Else are they very wretched.

Rosalind. Peace, I say...Good even to you, friend.

Corin. And to you, gentle sir, and to you all.

Rosalind. I prithee, shepherd, if that love or gold
Can in this desert place buy entertainment,
70 Bring us where we may rest ourselves and feed:
Here's a young maid with travel much oppressed,
And faints for succour.

Corin.   Fair sir, I pity her,
And wish, for her sake more than for mine own,
My fortunes were more able to relieve her:
But I am shepherd to another man,
And do not shear the fleeces that I graze:
My master is of churlish disposition,
And little recks to find the way to heaven
By doing deeds of hospitality:
80 Besides, his cote, his flocks and bounds of feed
Are now on sale, and at our sheepcote now
By reason of his absence there is nothing
That you will feed on; but what is, come see,
And in my voice most welcome shall you be.

Rosalind. What is he that shall buy his flock
    and pasture?

Corin. That young swain that you saw here
    but erewhile,
That little cares for buying any thing.

Rosalind. I pray thee, if it stand with honesty,
Buy thou the cottage, pasture, and the flock,
90 And thou shalt have to pay for it of us.

Celia. And we will mend thy wages: I like this place,
And willingly could waste my time in it.

Corin. Assuredly, the thing is to be sold...
Go with me. If you like upon report
The soil, the profit, and this kind of life,
I will your very faithful feeder be,
And buy it with your gold right suddenly.
              [*he goes; they rise and follow him*

[2. 5.]   *Before the cave of the exiled Duke*

'*AMIENS, JAQUES and others,*' *seated beneath the tree*

Amiens [*sings*]. Under the greenwood tree,
      Who loves to lie with me,
      And turn his merry note
      Unto the sweet bird's throat...
   Come hither, come hither, come hither:
      Here shall he see
      No enemy,
  But winter and rough weather.

Jaques. More, more, I prithee, more.

Amiens. It will make you melancholy, Monsieur 10
Jaques.

Jaques. I thank it...More, I prithee, more. I can
suck melancholy out of a song, as a weasel sucks eggs...
More, I prithee, more.

Amiens. My voice is ragged, I know I cannot please you.

Jaques. I do not desire you to please me, I do desire
you to sing...Come, more, another stanzo: call you 'em
stanzos?

Amiens. What you will, Monsieur Jaques.

Jaques. Nay, I care not for their names, they owe me 20
nothing....Will you sing?

Amiens. More at your request than to please myself.

Jaques. Well then, if ever I thank any man, I'll thank
you: but that they call compliment is like th'encounter
of two dog-apes; and when a man thanks me heartily,
methinks I have given him a penny and he renders me
the beggarly thanks....Come, sing; and you that will
not, hold your tongues.

Amiens. Well, I'll end the song....Sirs, cover the
while—the duke will drink under this tree...He hath 30
been all this day to look you.

   [*Some of the company prepare a meal beneath the tree*

Jaques. And I have been all this day to avoid him...
He is too disputable for my company...I think of as
many matters as he, but I give heaven thanks, and make
no boast of them....Come, warble, come.

They sing 'altogether here'

Who doth ambition shun,
And loves to live i'th' sun...
Seeking the food he eats,
And pleased with what he gets...
40   Come hither, come hither, come hither:
Here shall he see
No enemy,
But winter and rough weather.

Jaques. I'll give you a verse to this note, that I made
yesterday in despite of my invention.

Amiens. And I'll sing it.

Jaques. Thus it goes: *[gives a paper to Amiens*
Amiens. If it do come to pass,
That any man turn ass...
Leaving his wealth and ease,
A stubborn will to please,
Ducdame, ducdame, ducdame:
Here shall he see,
Gross fools as he,
An if he will come to me.
What's that 'ducdame'?

Jaques. 'Tis a Greek invocation, to call fools into a
circle....I'll go sleep, if I can: if I cannot, I'll rail
against all the first-born of Egypt.

Amiens. And I'll go seek the duke; his banquet is
prepared.   *[they depart in different directions*

[2. 6.] *The clearing in the outskirts of the forest*

ORLANDO *and* ADAM *approach*

Adam. Dear master, I can go no further: O, I die for food....[*he falls*] Here lie I down, and measure out my grave....Farewell, kind master.

Orlando. Why, how now, Adam! no greater heart in thee? Live a little, comfort a little, cheer thyself a little. If this uncouth forest yield any thing savage, I will either be food for it or bring it for food to thee...Thy conceit is nearer death than thy powers....[*he lifts him tenderly and props him against a tree*] For my sake be comfortable—hold death awhile at the arm's end: I will here be 10 with thee presently, and if I bring thee not something to eat, I will give thee leave to die: but if thou diest before I come, thou art a mocker of my labour....[*Adam murmurs some words*] Well said! thou look'st cheerly, and I'll be with thee quickly...Yet thou liest in the bleak air....[*he takes him in his arms*] Come, I will bear thee to some shelter—and thou shalt not die for lack of a dinner, if there live any thing in this desert....Cheerly, good Adam! [*he carries him away*

[2. 7.]   *Before the cave of the exiled Duke*

A meal of fruit and wine set out under the tree; the
DUKE *and some of his lords reclining thereat*

Duke. I think he be transformed into a beast,
For I can no where find him like a man.

First Lord. My lord, he is but even now gone hence,
Here was he merry, hearing of a song.

Duke. If he, compact of jars, grow musical,
We shall have shortly discord in the spheres:
Go, seek him, tell him I would speak with him.

JAQUES is seen coming through the trees, a smile upon his face, and shortly behind him AMIENS, who silently takes his seat next to the Duke at the meal when he comes up

   First Lord. He saves my labour by his own approach.
   Duke. Why, how now, monsieur! what a life is this,
10 That your poor friends must woo your company?
What, you look merrily!
   Jaques [*breaks into laughter*]. A fool, a fool! I met a
     fool i'th' forest,
A motley fool—a miserable world!—
As I do live by food, I met a fool,
Who laid him down and basked him in the sun,
And railed on Lady Fortune in good terms,
In good set terms, and yet a motley fool....
'Good morrow, fool,' quoth I: 'No, sir,' quoth he,
'Call me not fool till heaven hath sent me fortune.'
20 And then he drew a dial from his poke,
And looking on it with lack-lustre eye,
Says very wisely, 'It is ten o'clock:
Thus we may see,' quoth he, 'how the world wags:
'Tis but an hour ago since it was nine,
And after one hour more 'twill be eleven,
And so from hour to hour, we ripe, and ripe,
And then from hour to hour, we rot, and rot—
And thereby hangs a tale.'...When I did hear
The motley fool thus moral on the time,
30 My lungs began to crow like chanticleer,
That fools should be so deep-contemplative;
And I did laugh, sans intermission,
An hour by his dial....O noble fool!
O worthy fool! Motley's the only wear.
   Duke. What fool is this?

Jaques. A worthy fool...one that hath been a courtier,
And says, if ladies be but young and fair,
They have the gift to know it: and in his brain,
Which is as dry as the remainder biscuit
After a voyage, he hath strange places crammed   40
With observation, the which he vents
In mangled forms....O, that I were a fool!
I am ambitious for a motley coat.
  Duke. Thou shalt have one.
  Jaques.   ·It is my only suit—
Provided that you weed your better judgements
Of all opinion that grows rank in them
That I am wise....I must have liberty
Withal, as large a charter as the wind,
To blow on whom I please, for so fools have:
And they that are most galléd with my folly,   50
They most must laugh: and why, sir, must they so?
The 'why' is plain as way to parish church:
He that a fool doth very wisely hit
Doth very foolishly, although he smart,
Not to seem senseless of the bob: if not,
The wise man's folly is anatomized
Even by the squand'ring glances of the fool....
Invest me in my motley; give me leave
To speak my mind, and I will through and through
Cleanse the foul body of th'infected world,   60
If they will patiently receive my medicine.
  Duke. Fie on thee! I can tell what thou wouldst do.
  Jaques. What, for a counter, would I do but
        good?
  Duke. Most mischievous foul sin, in chiding sin:
For thou thyself hast been a libertine,
As sensual as the brutish sting itself,
And all th'embosséd sores and headed evils,

That thou with licence of free foot hast caught,
Wouldst thou disgorge into the general world.

70   *Jaques.* Why, who cries out on pride,
That can therein tax any private party?
Doth it not flow as hugely as the sea,
†Till that the weary very means do ebb?
What woman in the city do I name,
When that I say the city-woman bears
The cost of princes on unworthy shoulders?
Who can come in and say that I mean her,
When such a one as she such is her neighbour?
Or what is he of basest function,

80   That says his bravery is not on my cost,
Thinking that I mean him, but therein suits
His folly to the mettle of my speech?
There then!—how then? what then? Let me see wherein
My tongue hath wronged him: if it do him right,
Then he hath wronged himself; if he be free,
Why then my taxing like a wild-goose flies,
Unclaimed of any man....But who comes here?

ORLANDO *appears before them, with his sword drawn*

Orlando. Forbear, and eat no more.
Jaques.   Why, I have eat none yet.
Orlando. Nor shalt not, till necessity be served.

90   *Jaques.* Of what kind should this cock come of?
Duke. Art thou thus boldened, man, by thy distress?
Or else a rude despiser of good manners,
That in civility thou seem'st so empty?
Orlando. You touched my vein at first. The
        thorny point
Of bare distress hath ta'en from me the show
Of smooth civility: yet am I inland bred,
And know some nurture...But forbear, I say,

He dies that touches any of this fruit
Till I and my affairs are answeréd.

   Jaques [*taking up a bunch of raisins*]. An you will 100
not be answered with reason, I must die.

   Duke. What would you have? Your gentleness
      shall force,
More than your force move us to gentleness.

   Orlando. I almost die for food, and let me have it.

   Duke. Sit down and feed, and welcome to our table.

   Orlando. Speak you so gently? Pardon me, I
      pray you—
I thought that all things had been savage here,
And therefore put I on the countenance
Of stern commandment. But whate'er you are
That in this desert inaccessible,   110
Under the shade of melancholy boughs,
Lose and neglect the creeping hours of time;
If ever you have looked on better days;
If ever been where bells have knolled to church;
If ever sat at any good man's feast;
If ever from your eyelids wiped a tear,
And know what 'tis to pity and be pitied,
Let gentleness my strong enforcement be:
In the which hope I blush, and hide my sword.

   Duke. True is it that we have seen better days,   120
And have with holy bell been knolled to church,
And sat at good men's feasts, and wiped our eyes
Of drops that sacred pity hath engendred:
And therefore sit you down in gentleness,
And take upon command what help we have
That to your wanting may be ministred.

   Orlando. Then but forbear your food a little while,
Whiles, like a doe, I go to find my fawn,
And give it food....There is an old poor man,

130 Who after me hath many a weary step
Limped in pure love: till he be first sufficed,
Oppressed with two weak evils, age and hunger,
I will not touch a bit.
  Duke.   Go find him out,
And we will nothing waste till you return.
  Orlando. I thank ye, and be blessed for your
   good comfort!   [*he goes*
  Duke. Thou seest we are not all alone unhappy:
This wide and universal theatre
Presents more woeful pageants than the scene
Wherein we play in.
  Jaques.   All the world's a stage,
140 And all the men and women merely players;
They have their exits and their entrances,
And one man in his time plays many parts,
His acts being seven ages....At first the infant,
Mewling and puking in the nurse's arms:
Then the whining school-boy, with his satchel
And shining morning face, creeping like snail
Unwillingly to school: and then the lover,
Sighing like furnace, with a woeful ballad
Made to his mistress' eyebrow: then a soldier,
150 Full of strange oaths and bearded like the pard,
Jealous in honour, sudden and quick in quarrel,
Seeking the bubble reputation
Even in the cannon's mouth: and then the justice,
In fair round belly with good capon lined,
With eyes severe and beard of formal cut,
Full of wise saws and modern instances,
And so he plays his part....The sixth age shifts
Into the lean and slippered pantaloon,
With spectacles on nose and pouch on side,
160 His youthful hose, well saved, a world too wide

For his shrunk shank, and his big manly voice,
Turning again toward childish treble, pipes
And whistles in his sound....Last scene of all,
That ends this strange eventful history,
Is second childishness, and mere oblivion,
Sans teeth, sans eyes, sans taste, sans every thing.

ORLANDO returns with ADAM in his arms

Duke. Welcome...Set down your venerable burden,
And let him feed.
Orlando. I thank you most for him.
Adam.   So had you need,
I scarce can speak to thank you for myself.   170
Duke. Welcome, fall to: I will not trouble you
As yet to question you about your fortunes:
Give us some music, and good cousin, sing.

Amiens sings.

> Blow, blow, thou winter wind,
> Thou art not so unkind
>   As man's ingratitude:
> Thy tooth is not so keen,
> Because thou art not seen,
>   Although thy breath be rude....
> Hey-ho, sing hey-ho, unto the green holly,   180
> Most friendship is feigning; most loving mere folly:
>   Then hey-ho, the holly,
>   This life is most jolly.
>
> Freeze, freeze, thou bitter sky,
> That dost not bite so nigh
>   As benefits forgot:
> Though thou the waters warp,
> Thy sting is not so sharp
>   As friend remembred not....

190   Hey-ho, sing hey-ho, unto the green holly,
            Most friendship is feigning; most loving mere folly:
                Then hey-ho, the holly,
                    This life is most jolly.

        Duke. If that you were the good Sir Rowland's son,
        As you have whispered faithfully you were,
        And as mine eye doth his effigies witness
        Most truly limned and living in your face,
        Be truly welcome hither: I am the duke
        That loved your father. The residue of your fortune,
200   Go to my cave and tell me....Good old man,
        Thou art right welcome as thy master is:
        Support him by the arm....Give me your hand,
        And let me all your fortunes understand.
                                            [*they enter the cave*

        [3. 1.]   *A room in the palace of Duke Frederick*

        Enter Duke FREDERICK, *lords, and* OLIVER, *guarded
                        by attendants*

            Duke Frederick. Not see him since? Sir, sir, that
                cannot be:
        But were I not the better part made mercy,
        I should not seek an absent argument
        Of my revenge, thou present: but look to it,
        Find out thy brother wheresoe'er he is—
        Seek him with candle; bring him dead or living
        Within this twelvemonth, or turn thou no more
        To seek a living in our territory....
        Thy lands and all things that thou dost call thine
10   Worth seizure do we seize into our hands,
        Till thou canst quit thee by thy brother's mouth
        Of what we think against thee.
            Oliver. O, that your highness knew my heart in this!
        I never loved my brother in my life.

Duke Frederick. More villain thou....Well, push him
    out of doors,
And let my officers of such a nature
Make an extent upon his house and lands:
Do this expediently and turn him going.   *[they go*

[3. 2.] *The clearing in the outskirts of the forest, near*
the sheepcote

ORLANDO *with a paper, which he fixes to*
the trunk of a tree

Orlando. Hang there, my verse, in witness of my love,
    And thou, thrice-crownéd queen of night, survey
With thy chaste eye, from thy pale sphere above,
    Thy huntress' name that my full life doth sway....
O Rosalind! these trees shall be my books,
    And in their barks my thoughts I'll character,
That every eye which in this forest looks
    Shall see thy virtue witnessed every where....
Run, run, Orlando, carve on every tree
The fair, the chaste and unexpressive she.   10
                     [he passes on

CORIN *and* TOUCHSTONE *come up*

Corin. And how like you this shepherd's life, Master
Touchstone?
Touchstone. Truly, shepherd, in respect of itself, it is
a good life; but in respect that it is a shepherd's life, it
is naught. In respect that it is solitary, I like it very well;
but in respect that it is private, it is a very vile life. Now
in respect it is in the fields, it pleaseth me well; but in
respect it is not in the court, it is tedious. As it is a spare
life, look you, it fits my humour well; but as there is no
more plenty in it, it goes much against my stomach. 20
Hast any philosophy in thee, shepherd?
Corin. No more, but that I know the more one

sickens, the worse at ease he is; and that he that wants
money, means and content is without three good
friends; that the property of rain is to wet and fire to
burn; that good pasture makes fat sheep; and that a
great cause of the night, is lack of the sun; that he
that hath learned no wit by nature nor art may complain of good breeding or comes of a very dull kindred.

30 *Touchstone*. Such a one is a natural philosopher...
Wast ever in court, shepherd?

Corin. No, truly.

Touchstone. Then thou art damned.

Corin. Nay, I hope.

Touchstone. Truly thou art damned, like an ill-
roasted egg all on one side.

Corin. For not being at court? Your reason.

Touchstone. Why, if thou never wast at court, thou
never saw'st good manners; if thou never saw'st good
40 manners, then thy manners must be wicked, and wicked-
ness is sin, and sin is damnation...Thou art in a parlous
state, shepherd.

Corin. Not a whit, Touchstone. Those that are good
manners at the court are as ridiculous in the country,
as the behaviour of the country is most mockable at the
court. You told me you salute not at the court, but you
kiss your hands; that courtesy would be uncleanly, if
courtiers were shepherds.

Touchstone. Instance, briefly; come, instance.

50 *Corin*. Why, we are still handling our ewes, and their
fells you know are greasy.

Touchstone. Why, do not your courtier's hands sweat?
and is not the grease of a mutton as wholesome as the
sweat of a man? Shallow, shallow: a better instance, I
say: come.

Corin. Besides, our hands are hard.

Touchstone. Your lips will feel them the sooner. Shallow, again: a more sounder instance, come.

Corin. And they are often tarred over with the surgery of our sheep; and would you have us kiss tar? The 60 courtier's hands are perfumed with civet.

Touchstone. Most shallow man! thou worms-meat, in respect of a good piece of flesh indeed! Learn of the wise, and perpend: civet is of a baser birth than tar, the very uncleanly flux of a cat. Mend the instance, shepherd.

Corin. You have too courtly a wit for me, I'll rest.

Touchstone. Wilt thou rest damned? God help thee, shallow man! God make incision in thee! thou art raw. 70

Corin. Sir, I am a true labourer. I earn that I eat, get that I wear, owe no man hate, envy no man's happiness, glad of other men's good, content with my harm; and the greatest of my pride is to see my ewes graze and my lambs suck.

Touchstone. That is another simple sin in you, to bring the ewes and the rams together, and to offer to get your living by the copulation of cattle—to be bawd to a bell-wether, and to betray a she-lamb of a twelvemonth to a crooked-pated, old, cuckoldly ram, out of all reason- 80 able match. If thou beest not damned for this, the devil himself will have no shepherds—I cannot see else how thou shouldst 'scape.

Corin. Here comes young Master Ganymede, my new mistress's brother.

ROSALIND, unwitting of their presence, comes up, sees ORLANDO'S paper on the tree and, plucking it down, begins to read it

Rosalind. 'From the east to western Ind,
          No jewel is like Rosalind.

Her worth, being mounted on the wind,
Through all the world bears Rosalind.
90   All the pictures fairest lined
Are but black to Rosalind....
Let no face be kept in mind
But the fair of Rosalind.'

Touchstone [*taps her on the arm with his bauble*]. I'll rhyme you so eight years together, dinners, and suppers, and sleeping-hours excepted: it is the right butter-women's rank to market.

Rosalind. Out, fool!

Touchstone. For a taste....
100   If a hart do lack a hind,
Let him seek out Rosalind:
If the cat will after kind,
So be sure will Rosalind:
Wintered garments must be lined,
So must slender Rosalind.
They that reap must sheaf and bind,
Then to cart with Rosalind.
Sweetest nut hath sourest rind,
Such a nut is Rosalind.
110   He that sweetest rose will find,
Must find love's prick and Rosalind.

This is the very false gallop of verses. Why do you infect yourself with them?

Rosalind. Peace, you dull fool! I found them on a tree.

Touchstone. Truly, the tree yields bad fruit.

Rosalind. I'll graff it with you, and then I shall graff it with a medlar: then it will be the earliest fruit i'th' country: for you'll be rotten ere you be half ripe, and 120 that's the right virtue of the medlar.

Touchstone. You have said: but whether wisely or no, let the forest judge.

CELIA draws near, likewise reading a paper

Rosalind. Peace!
Here comes my sister, reading. Stand aside.
                      [*they hide behind a tree*

Celia. 'Why should this a desert be?
     For it is unpeopled? No;
   Tongues I'll hang on every tree,
     That shall civil sayings show.
   Some, how brief the life of man
     Runs his erring pilgrimage,   130
   That the stretching of a span
     Buckles in his sum of age;
   Some, of violated vows
     'Twixt the souls of friend and friend:
   But upon the fairest boughs,
     Or at every sentence end,
   Will I Rosalinda write,
     Teaching all that read to know
   The quintessence of every sprite
     Heaven would in little show.   140
   Therefore Heaven Nature charged,
     That one body should be filled
   With all graces wide-enlarged:
     Nature presently distilled
   Helen's cheek, but not her heart,
     Cleopatra's majesty,
   Atalanta's better part,
     Sad Lucretia's modesty....
   Thus Rosalind of many parts
     By heavenly synod was devised,   150
   Of many faces, eyes, and hearts,
     To have the touches dearest prized....
Heaven would that she these gifts should have,
And I to live and die her slave.'

Rosalind. O most gentle pulpiter, what tedious homily of love have you wearied your parishioners withal, and never cried, 'Have patience, good people!'

Celia [*starts and turns, dropping the paper*]. How now, back-friends! Shepherd, go off a little....Go with 160 him, sirrah.

Touchstone. Come, shepherd, let us make an honourable retreat—though not with bag and baggage, yet with. scrip and scrippage.

[*Touchstone picks up the verses and departs with Corin*
Celia. Didst thou hear these verses?

Rosalind. O, yes, I heard them all, and more too, for some of them had in them more feet than the verses would bear.

Celia. That's no matter: the feet might bear the verses.

Rosalind. Ay, but the feet were lame, and could not 170 bear themselves without the verse, and therefore stood lamely in the verse.

Celia. But didst thou hear without wondering how thy name should be hanged and carved upon these trees?

Rosalind. I was seven of the nine days out of the wonder before you came; for look here what I found on a palm-tree...I was never so be-rhymed since Pythagoras' time, that I was an Irish rat, which I can hardly remember.

Celia. Trow you who hath done this?

180 *Rosalind.* Is it a man?

Celia. And a chain that you once wore about his neck! Change you colour?

Rosalind. I prithee, who?

Celia. O Lord, Lord! it is a hard matter for friends to meet; but mountains may be removed with earthquakes and so encounter.

Rosalind. Nay, but who is it?

Celia. Is it possible?

Rosalind. Nay, I prithee now with most petitionary
vehemence, tell me who it is.   190

Celia. O wonderful, wonderful, and most wonderful
wonderful! and yet again wonderful, and after that out
of all whooping!

Rosalind. Good my complexion! dost thou think,
though I am caparisoned like a man, I have a doublet-
and-hose in my disposition? One inch of delay more is
a South-sea of discovery....I prithee, tell me who is it
quickly, and speak apace: I would thou couldst stammer,
that thou mightst pour this concealed man out of thy
mouth, as wine comes out of a narrow-mouthed bottle; 200
either too much at once, or none at all. I prithee take the
cork out of thy mouth that I may drink thy tidings.

Celia. So you may put a man in your belly.

Rosalind. Is he of God's making? What manner of man?
Is his head worth a hat? or his chin worth a beard?

Celia. Nay, he hath but a little beard.

Rosalind. Why, God will send more, if the man will
be thankful: let me stay the growth of his beard, if thou
delay me not the knowledge of his chin.

Celia. It is young Orlando, that tripped up the 210
wrestler's heels, and your heart, both in an instant.

Rosalind. Nay, but the devil take mocking; speak sad
brow and true maid.

Celia. I'faith, coz, 'tis he.

Rosalind. Orlando?

Celia. Orlando.

Rosalind. Alas the day, what shall I do with my doublet
and hose? What did he when thou saw'st him? What
said he? How looked he? Wherein went he? What
makes he here? Did he ask for me? Where remains he? 220
How parted he with thee? and when shalt thou see him
again? Answer me in one word.

Celia. You must borrow me Gargantua's mouth first: 'tis a word too great for any mouth of this age's size. To say ay and no to these particulars is more than to answer in a catechism.

Rosalind. But doth he know that I am in this forest and in man's apparel? Looks he as freshly as he did the day he wrestled?

230 *Celia.* It is as easy to count atomies as to resolve the propositions of a lover: but take a taste of my finding him, and relish it with a good observance. I found him under a tree, like a dropped acorn.

Rosalind. It may well be called Jove's tree, when it †drops forth such fruit.

Celia. Give me audience, good madam.

Rosalind. Proceed.

Celia. There lay he, stretched along, like a wounded knight:

240 *Rosalind.* Though it be pity to see such a sight, it well becomes the ground.

Celia. Cry 'holla' to thy tongue, I prithee; it curvets unseasonably....He was furnished like a hunter.

Rosalind. O ominous! he comes to kill my heart.

Celia. I would sing my song without a burden—thou bring'st me out of tune.

Rosalind. Do you not know I am a woman? when I think, I must speak...Sweet, say on.

ORLANDO *and* JAQUES *are seen coming through the trees*

Celia. You bring me out....Soft! comes he not here?

250 *Rosalind.* 'Tis he—slink by, and note him.

[*Celia and Rosalind steal behind a tree, within earshot*

Jaques. I thank you for your company—but, good faith,
I had as lief have been myself alone.

Orlando. And so had I: but yet, for fashion sake,
I thank you too for your society.

Jaques. God buy you, let's meet as little as we can.

Orlando. I do desire we may be better strangers.

Jaques. I pray you, mar no more trees with writing
love-songs in their barks.

Orlando. I pray you, mar no moe of my verses with
reading them ill-favouredly.   260

Jaques. Rosalind is your love's name?

Orlando. Yes, just.

Jaques. I do not like her name.

Orlando. There was no thought of pleasing you when
she was christened.

Jaques. What stature is she of?

Orlando. Just as high as my heart.

Jaques. You are full of pretty answers: have you not
been acquainted with goldsmiths' wives, and conned
them out of rings?   270

Orlando. Not so; but I answer you right painted cloth,
from whence you have studied your questions.

Jaques. You have a nimble wit; I think 'twas made
of Atalanta's heels....Will you sit down with me? and
we two will rail against our mistress the world, and all
our misery.

Orlando. I will chide no breather in the world but
myself, against whom I know most faults.

Jaques. The worst fault you have is to be in love.

Orlando. 'Tis a fault I will not change for your   280
best virtue...I am weary of you.

Jaques. By my troth, I was seeking for a fool when
I found you.

Orlando. He is drowned in the brook—look but in,
and you shall see him.

Jaques. There I shall see mine own figure.

Orlando. Which I take to be either a fool or a cipher.

Jaques. I'll tarry no longer with you. Farewell, good
290 Signior Love.   [*he bows*

Orlando. I am glad of your departure: [*he bows like-wise*] adieu, good Monsieur Melancholy.

[*Jaques departs*

(*Rosalind.* I will speak to him like a saucy lackey, and under that habit play the knave with him.
[*calls*] Do you hear, forester?

Orlando [*turns*]. Very well. What would you?

Rosalind. I pray you, what is't o'clock?

Orlando. You should ask me what time o'day: there's no clock in the forest.

300 *Rosalind.* Then there is no true lover in the forest, else sighing every minute and groaning every hour would detect the lazy foot of Time as well as a clock.

Orlando. And why not the swift foot of Time? had not that been as proper?

Rosalind. By no means, sir: Time travels in divers paces with divers persons...I'll tell you who Time ambles withal, who Time trots withal, who Time gallops withal, and who he stands still withal.

Orlando. I prithee, who doth he trot withal?

310 *Rosalind.* Marry, he trots hard with a young maid between the contract of her marriage and the day it is solemnized: if the interim be but a se'nnight, Time's pace is so hard that it seems the length of seven year.

Orlando. Who ambles Time withal?

Rosalind. With a priest that lacks Latin, and a rich man that hath not the gout: for the one sleeps easily because he cannot study, and the other lives merrily because he feels no pain: the one lacking the burden of

lean and wasteful learning; the other knowing no burden 320
of heavy tedious penury....These Time ambles withal.

Orlando. Who doth he gallop withal?

Rosalind. With a thief to the gallows: for though he
go as softly as foot can fall, he thinks himself too soon
there.

Orlando. Who stays it still withal?

Rosalind. With lawyers in the vacation: for they sleep
between term and term, and then they perceive not how
Time moves.

Orlando. Where dwell you, pretty youth? 330

Rosalind. With this shepherdess, my sister; here in the
skirts of the forest, like fringe upon a petticoat.

Orlando. Are you native of this place?

Rosalind. As the cony that you see dwell where she
is kindled.

Orlando. Your accent is something finer than you
could purchase in so removed a dwelling.

Rosalind. I have been told so of many: but indeed an
old religious uncle of mine taught me to speak, who was
in his youth an inland man—one that knew courtship 340
too well, for there he fell in love....I have heard him
read many lectures against it, and I thank God I am
not a woman, to be touched with so many giddy offences
as he hath generally taxed their whole sex withal.

Orlando. Can you remember any of the principal evils
that he laid to the charge of women?

Rosalind. There were none principal, they were all
like one another as half-pence are, every one fault
seeming monstrous till his fellow-fault came to match it.

Orlando. I prithee, recount some of them. 350

Rosalind. No: I will not cast away my physic but on
those that are sick....There is a man haunts the forest,
that abuses our young plants with carving 'Rosalind' on

their barks; hangs odes upon hawthorns and elegies on
brambles; all, forsooth, deifying the name of Rosalind:
if I could meet that fancy-monger, I would give him
some good counsel, for he seems to have the quotidian
of love upon him.

Orlando. I am he that is so love-shaked. I pray you,
tell me your remedy.

Rosalind. There is none of my uncle's marks upon
you: he taught me how to **know a** man in love; in which
cage of rushes I am sure **you are not** prisoner.

Orlando. What were his **marks?**

Rosalind. A lean cheek, which you have not: a blue
eye and sunken, which you have not: an unquestionable
spirit, which you have not: a beard neglected, which
you have not...but I pardon you for that, for simply
your having in beard is a younger brother's revenue.
Then your hose should be ungartered, your bonnet unbanded, your sleeve unbuttoned, your shoe untied, and
every thing about you demonstrating a careless desolation: but you are no such man; you are rather point-
device in your accoutrements, as loving yourself than
seeming the lover of any other.

Orlando. Fair youth, I would I could make thee believe I love.

Rosalind. Me believe it! you may as soon make her
that you love believe it, which I warrant she is apter to
do than to confess she does: that is one of the points in
the which women still give the lie to their consciences....
But, in good sooth, are you he that hangs the verses on
the trees, wherein Rosalind is so admired?

Orlando. I swear to thee, youth, by the white hand of
Rosalind, I am that he, that unfortunate he.

Rosalind. But are you so much in love as your rhymes
speak?

Orlando. Neither rhyme nor reason can express how much.

Rosalind. Love is merely a madness, and I tell you 390 deserves as well a dark house and a whip as madmen do: and the reason why they are not so punished and cured is, that the lunacy is so ordinary that the whippers are in love too...Yet I profess curing it by counsel.

Orlando. Did you ever cure any so?

Rosalind. Yes, one, and in this manner. He was to imagine me his love, his mistress; and I set him every day to woo me: at which time would I, being but a moonish youth, grieve, be effeminate, changeable, long- 400 ing and liking, proud, fantastical, apish, shallow, inconstant, full of tears, full of smiles; for every passion something, and for no passion truly any thing, as boys and women are for the most part cattle of this colour: would now like him, now loath him; then entertain him, then forswear him; now weep for him, then spit at him; that I drave my suitor from his mad humour of love to a living humour of madness—which was, to forswear the full stream of the world and to live in a nook merely monastic...And thus I cured him, and this way 410 will I take upon me to wash your liver as clean as a sound sheep's heart, that there shall not be one spot of love in't.

Orlando. I would not be cured, youth.

Rosalind. I would cure you, if you would but call me Rosalind, and come every day to my cote, and woo me.

Orlando. Now, by the faith of my love, I will...Tell me where it is.

Rosalind. Go with me to it, and I'll show it you: and by the way you shall tell me where in the forest you 420 live...Will you go?

Orlando. With all my heart, good youth.

Rosalind. Nay, you must call me Rosalind...Come, sister, will you go?   [*they go*

Some days pass

[3. 3.] *The clearing near the sheepcote (as before)*

TOUCHSTONE *and* AUDREY *approach;* JAQUES
following at a little distance

Touchstone. Come apace, good Audrey. I will fetch up your goats, Audrey...And how, Audrey? am I the man yet? Doth my simple feature content you?

Audrey. Your features, Lord warrant us! what features?

Touchstone. I am here with thee and thy goats, as the most capricious poet, honest Ovid, was among the Goths.

(*Jaques.* O knowledge ill-inhabited! worse than Jove in a thatched house!

10 *Touchstone.* When a man's verses cannot be understood, nor a man's good wit seconded with the forward child, understanding, it strikes a man more dead than a great reckoning in a little room....Truly, I would the gods had made thee poetical.

Audrey. I do not know what 'poetical' is: is it honest in deed and word? is it a true thing?

Touchstone. No, truly; for the truest poetry is the most feigning; and lovers are given to poetry; and what they swear in poetry it may be said as lovers they do feign.

20 *Audrey.* Do you wish then that the gods had made me poetical?

Touchstone. I do, truly: for thou swear'st to me thou art honest; now, if thou wert a poet, I might have some hope thou didst feign.

Audrey. Would you not have me honest?

Touchstone. No, truly, unless thou wert hard-favoured: for honesty coupled to beauty is to have honey a sauce to sugar.

(*Jaques.* A material fool!

Audrey. Well, I am not fair, and therefore I pray the 30 gods make me honest.

Touchstone. Truly, and to cast away honesty upon a foul slut were to put good meat into an unclean dish.

Audrey. I am not a slut, though I thank the gods I am foul.

Touchstone. Well, praised be the gods for thy foulness! sluttishness may come hereafter....But be it as it may be, I will marry thee: and to that end, I have been with Sir Oliver Martext the vicar of the next village, who 40 hath promised to meet me in this place of the forest and to couple us.

(*Jaques.* I would fain see this meeting.

Audrey. Well, the gods give us joy!

Touchstone. Amen....A man may, if he were of a fearful heart, stagger in this attempt; for here we have no temple but the wood, no assembly but horn-beasts. But what though? Courage! As horns are odious, they are necessary. It is said, 'many a man knows no end of his goods': right; many a man has good horns, and 50 knows no end of them. Well, that is the dowry of his wife; 'tis none of his own getting...Horns? Even so. Poor men alone? No, no, the noblest deer hath them as huge as the rascal...Is the single man therefore blessed? No, as a walled town is more worthier than a village, so is the forehead of a married man more honourable than the bare brow of a bachelor: and by how much defence is better than no skill, by so much is a horn more precious than to want....

SIR OLIVER MARTEXT comes up

50 Here comes Sir Oliver...Sir Oliver Martext, you are well met. Will you dispatch us here under this tree, or shall we go with you to your chapel?

Sir Oliver Martext. Is there none here to give the woman?

Touchstone. I will not take her on gift of any man.

Sir Oliver Martext. Truly, she must be given, or the marriage is not lawful.

Jaques [*comes forward, doffing his hat*]. Proceed, proceed; I'll give her.

70 *Touchstone.* Good even, good Master What-ye-call't: how do you, sir? You are very well met: God'ild you for your last company—I am very glad to see you—even a toy in hand here, sir...Nay, pray be covered.

Jaques. Will you be married, motley?

Touchstone. As the ox hath his bow, sir, the horse his curb, and the falcon her bells, so man hath his desires; and as pigeons bill, so wedlock would be nibbling.

Jaques. And will you, being a man of your breeding, be married under a bush like a beggar? Get you to 80 church, and have a good priest that can tell you what marriage is—this fellow will but join you together as they join wainscot, then one of you will prove a shrunk panel, and like green timber warp, warp.

Touchstone. I am not in the mind but I were better to be married of him than of another, for he is not like to marry me well...and not being well married, it will be a good excuse for me hereafter to leave my wife.

Jaques. Go thou with me, and let me counsel thee.

Touchstone. Come, sweet Audrey,

90 We must be married, or we must live in bawdry...
Farewell, good Master Oliver: not— [*sings and dances*

> O sweet Oliver,
> O brave Oliver,
> Leave me not behind thee:

but—

> Wind away,
> Begone, I say,
> I will not to wedding with thee.

[he dances off, Jaques and Audrey following Sir Oliver Martext. 'Tis no matter; ne'er a fantastical knave of them all shall flout me out of my calling.   100

[he goes

[3. 4.] *ROSALIND and CELIA come along the path from the cottage; Rosalind drops upon a bank*

Rosalind. Never talk to me, I will weep.

Celia. Do, I prithee—but yet have the grace to consider that tears do not become a man.

Rosalind. But have I not cause to weep?

Celia. As good cause as one would desire, therefore weep.

Rosalind. His very hair is of the dissembling colour.

Celia. Something browner than Judas's: marry, his kisses are Judas's own children.

Rosalind. I'faith, his hair is of a good colour.   10

Celia. An excellent colour: your chestnut was ever the only colour.

Rosalind. And his kissing is as full of sanctity as the touch of holy bread.

Celia. He hath bought a pair of cast lips of Diana: a nun of winter's sisterhood kisses not more religiously, the very ice of chastity is in them.

Rosalind. But why did he swear he would come this morning, and comes not?

Celia. Nay, certainly, there is no truth in him.   20

Rosalind. Do you think so?

Celia. Yes, I think he is not a pick-purse nor a horse-stealer, but for his verity in love I do think him as concave as a covered goblet or a worm-eaten nut.

Rosalind. Not true in love?

Celia. Yes, when he is in—but I think he is not in.

Rosalind. You have heard him swear downright he was.

Celia. 'Was' is not 'is': besides, the oath of a lover
30 is no stronger than the word of a tapster, they are both the confirmer of false reckonings. He attends here in the forest on the duke your father.

Rosalind. I met the duke yesterday and had much question with him: he asked me of what parentage I was; I told him, of as good as he—so he laughed and let me go....But what talk we of fathers, when there is such a man as Orlando?

Celia. O, that's a brave man! he writes brave verses, speaks brave words, swears brave oaths and breaks
40 them bravely, quite traverse, athwart the heart of his lover—as a puny tilter, that spurs his horse but on one side, breaks his staff like a noble goose; but all's brave that youth mounts and folly guides....Who comes here?

CORIN *draws near and accosts them*

Corin. Mistress and master, you have oft inquired
After the shepherd that complained of love,
Who you saw sitting by me on the turf,
Praising the proud disdainful shepherdess
That was his mistress.

Celia.   Well: and what of him?

Corin. If you will see a pageant truly played,
50 Between the pale complexion of true love
And the red glow of scorn and proud disdain,

Go hence a little and I shall conduct you,
If you will mark it.

   Rosalind.   O, come, let us remove.
The sight of lovers feedeth those in love:
Bring us to this sight, and you shall say
I'll prove a busy actor in their play..   *[they go*

[3. 5.]   *Another part of the forest*

  PHEBE, followed by SILVIUS who entreats her

 Silvius [kneels]. Sweet Phebe, do not scorn me, do
    not, Phebe:
Say that you love me not, but say not so
In bitterness...The common executioner,
Whose heart th'accustomed sight of death makes hard,
Falls not the axe upon the humbled neck
But first begs pardon: will you sterner be
Than he that dies and lives by bloody drops?

  ROSALIND, CELIA, and CORIN come up behind, unseen

 Phebe. I would not be thy executioner.
I fly thee, for I would not injure thee...
Thou tell'st me there is murder in mine eye—   10
'Tis pretty, sure, and very probable,
That eyes, that are the frail'st and softest things,
Who shut their coward gates on atomies,
Should be called tyrants, butchers, murderers!
Now I do frown on thee with all my heart,
And if mine eyes can wound, now let them kill thee;
Now counterfeit to swoon, why now fall down,
Or if thou canst not, O for shame, for shame,
Lie not, to say mine eyes are murderers!
Now show the wound mine eye hath made in thee.   20
Scratch thee but with a pin, and there remains
Some scar of it: lean upon a rush,

The cicatrice and capable impressure
Thy palm some moment keeps: but now mine eyes,
Which I have darted at thee, hurt thee not,
Nor, I am sure, there is no force in eyes
That can do hurt.

 Silvius.   O dear Phebe,
If ever—as that ever may be near—
You meet in some fresh cheek the power of fancy,
30 Then shall you know the wounds invisible
That love's keen arrows make.

 Phebe.   But till that time
Come not thou near me: and when that time comes,
Afflict me with thy mocks, pity me not,
As till that time I shall not pity thee.

 Rosalind [*advancing*]. And why, I pray you? Who
   might be your mother,
That you insult, exult, and all at once,
Over the wretched? What though you have no beauty—
As, by my faith, I see no more in you
Than without candle may go dark to bed—
40 Must you be therefore proud and pitiless?
Why, what means this? Why do you look on me?
I see no more in you than in the ordinary
Of nature's sale-work! 'Od's my little life,
I think she means to tangle my eyes too:
No, faith, proud mistress, hope not after it.
'Tis not your inky brows, your black silk hair,
Your bugle eyeballs, nor your cheek of cream,
That can entame my spirits to your worship...
You foolish shepherd, wherefore do you follow her,
50 Like foggy south, puffing with wind and rain?
You are a thousand times a properer man
Than she a woman: 'tis such fools as you
That makes the world full of ill-favoured children:

'Tis not her glass, but you, that flatters her,
And out of you she sees herself more proper
Than any of her lineaments can show her...
But, mistress, know yourself—down on your knees,
And thank heaven, fasting, for a good man's love;

　　　　　　　　　　[*Phebe kneels to Rosalind*

For I must tell you friendly in your ear,
Sell when you can—you are not for all markets:　　60
Cry the man mercy, love him, take his offer.
Foul is most foul, being foul to be a scoffer....
So take her to thee, shepherd—fare you well.
　Phebe. Sweet youth, I pray you chide a year together.
I had rather hear you chide than this man woo.
　Rosalind [*to Phebe*]. He's fallen in love with your
foulness, [*to Silvius*] and she'll fall in love with my
anger. If it be so, as fast as she answers thee with
frowning looks, I'll sauce her with bitter words...[*to
Phebe*] Why look you so upon me?　　70
　Phebe. For no ill will I bear you.
　Rosalind. I pray you, do not fall in love with me,
For I am falser than vows made in wine:
Besides, I like you not...If you will know my house,
'Tis at the tuft of olives here hard by...
Will you go, sister? Shepherd, ply her hard...
Come, sister...Shepherdess, look on him better,
And be not proud—though all the world could see,
None could be so abused in sight as he....
Come, to our flock.　　80
　　　　　[*she stalks away followed by Celia and Corin*
　Phebe [*gazing after them*]. Dead Shepherd, now I
　　find thy saw of might,
'Who ever loved that loved not at first sight?'
　Silvius. Sweet Phebe—
　Phebe.　　　　　　　　Ha! what say'st thou, Silvius?

Silvius. Sweet Phebe, pity me.

Phebe. Why, I am sorry for thee, gentle Silvius.

Silvius. Wherever sorrow is, relief would be:
If you do sorrow at my grief in love,
By giving love your sorrow and my grief
Were both extermined.

90   *Phebe.* Thou hast my love—is not that neighbourly?

Silvius. I would have you.

Phebe.   Why, that were covetousness...
Silvius, the time was that I hated thee,
And yet it is not that I bear thee love;
But since that thou canst talk of love so well,
Thy company, which erst was irksome to me,
I will endure; and I'll employ thee too:
But do not look for further recompense
Than thine own gladness that thou art employed.

Silvius. So holy and so perfect is my love,

100 And I in such a poverty of grace,
That I shall think it a most plenteous crop
To glean the broken ears after the man
That the main harvest reaps: loose now and then
A scattered smile, and that I'll live upon.

Phebe. Know'st thou the youth that spoke to me
     erewhile?

Silvius. Not very well, but I have met him oft,
And he hath bought the cottage and the bounds
That the old carlot once was master of.

Phebe. Think not I love him, though I ask for him.

110 'Tis but a peevish boy—yet he talks well—
But what care I for words?—yet words do well,
When he, that speaks them pleases those that hear:
It is a pretty youth—not very pretty—
But, sure, he's proud—and yet his pride becomes him:
He'll make a proper man: the best thing in him

Is his complexion; and faster than his tongue
Did make offence, his eye did heal it up:
He is not very tall—yet for his years he's tall:
His leg is but so so—and yet 'tis well:
There was a pretty redness in his lip,　　　　　120
A little riper and more lusty red
Than that mixed in his cheek; 'twas just the difference
Betwixt the constant red and mingled damask....
There be some women, Silvius, had they marked him
In parcels as I did, would have gone near
To fall in love with him: but, for my part,
I love him not, nor hate him not; and yet
I have more cause to hate him than to love him,
For what had he to do to chide at me?
He said mine eyes were black and my hair black,　　　130
And, now I am remembered, scorn'd at me:
I marvel why I answered not again:
But that's all one; omittance is no quittance:
I'll write to him a very taunting letter,
And thou shalt bear it—wilt thou, Silvius?
　Silvius. Phebe, with all my heart.
　Phebe.　　　　　　　　I'll write it straight;
The matter's in my head and in my heart.
I will be bitter with him and passing short:
Go with me, Silvius.　　　　　　　*[they go*

[4. 1.]　　　*The clearing near the sheepcote*

Enter ROSALIND, CELIA, *and* JAQUES

　Jaques. I prithee, pretty youth, let me be better
acquainted with thee.
　Rosalind. They say you are a melancholy fellow.
　Jaques. I am so: I do love it better than laughing.
　Rosalind. Those that are in extremity of either are

abominable fellows, and betray themselves to every
modern censure worse than drunkards.

Jaques. Why, 'tis good to be sad and say nothing.

Rosalind. Why then, 'tis good to be a post.

10 *Jaques.* I have neither the scholar's melancholy,
which is emulation; nor the musician's, which is fantastical; nor the courtier's, which is proud; nor the
soldier's, which is ambitious; nor the lawyer's, which is
politic; nor the lady's, which is nice; nor the lover's,
which is all these: but it is a melancholy of mine own,
compounded of many simples, extracted from many
objects, and indeed the sundry contemplation of my
travels, in which my often rumination wraps me in a
most humorous sadness.

20 *Rosalind.* A traveller! By my faith, you have great
reason to be sad: I fear you have sold your own lands
to see other men's; then, to have seen much, and to have
nothing, is to have rich eyes and poor hands.

Jaques. Yes, I have gained my experience.

ORLANDO *draws near*

Rosalind. And your experience makes you sad: I had
rather have a fool to make me merry than experience
to make me sad—and to travel for it too!

Orlando. Good day, and happiness, dear Rosalind!

[*she takes no heed of him*

Jaques. Nay then, God buy you, an you talk in blank
30 verse.   [*he turns from them*

Rosalind. Farewell, Monsieur Traveller: look you
lisp and wear strange suits; disable all the benefits of
your own country; be out of love with your nativity,
and almost chide God for making you that countenance
you are; or I will scarce think you have swam in a
gondola....[*Jaques passes out of earshot; she sits*] Why,

how now, Orlando! where have you been all this while?
You a lover! An you serve me such another trick, never
come in my sight more.

Orlando. My fair Rosalind, I come within an hour of 40
my promise.

Rosalind. Break an hour's promise in love? He that
will divide a minute into a thousand parts, and break
but a part of the thousandth part of a minute in the
affairs of love, it may be said of him that Cupid hath
clapped him o'th' shoulder, but I'll warrant him heart-
whole.

Orlando. Pardon me, dear Rosalind.

Rosalind. Nay, an you be so tardy come no more in
my sight, I had as lief be wooed of a snail.   50

Orlando. Of a snail?

Rosalind. Ay, of a snail; for though he comes slowly,
he carries his house on his head; a better jointure, I
think, than you make a woman: besides, he brings his
destiny with him.

Orlando. What's that?   [*he sits beside her*

Rosalind. Why, horns; which such as you are fain to
be beholding to your wives for: but he comes armed in
his fortune, and prevents the slander of his wife.

Orlando. Virtue is no horn-maker...[*musing*] and my 60
Rosalind is virtuous.

Rosalind. And I am your Rosalind.

                    [*she puts her arm about his neck*

Celia. It pleases him to call you so; but he hath a
Rosalind of a better leer than you.

Rosalind. Come, woo me, woo me; for now I am in a
holiday humour, and like enough to consent...What
would you say to me now, an I were your very very
Rosalind?

Orlando. I would kiss before I spoke.

70 *Rosalind.* Nay, you were better speak first, and when
you were gravelled for lack of matter, you might take
occasion to kiss: very good orators, when they are out,
they will spit, and for lovers, lacking (God warr'nt us!)
matter, the cleanliest shift is to kiss.

Orlando. How if the kiss be denied?

Rosalind. Then she puts you to entreaty and there
begins new matter.

Orlando. Who could be out, being before his beloved
mistress?

80 *Rosalind.* Marry, that should you if I were your mistress, or I should think my honesty ranker than my wit.

Orlando. What, of my suit?

Rosalind. Not out of your apparel, and yet out of your
suit...Am not I your Rosalind?

Orlando. I take some joy to say you are, because I
would be talking of her.

Rosalind. Well, in her person, I say I will not have
you.

Orlando. Then in mine own person, I die.

90 *Rosalind.* No, faith, die by attorney: the poor world
is almost six thousand years old, and in all this time
there was not any man died in his own person, videlicet,
in a love-cause: Troilus had his brains dashed out with
a Grecian club, yet he did what he could to die before,
and he is one of the patterns of love: Leander, he would
have lived many a fair year, though Hero had turned
nun, if it had not been for a hot midsummer night; for,
good youth, he went but forth to wash him in the
Hellespont and being taken with the cramp was drowned,

100 and the foolish chroniclers of that age found it was
'Hero of Sestos.'....But these are all lies. Men have
died from time to time, and worms have eaten them,
but not for love.

Orlando. I would not have my right Rosalind of this mind, for I protest her frown might kill me.

Rosalind. By this hand, it will not kill a fly...[*draws closer to him*] But come, now I will be your Rosalind in a more coming-on disposition; and ask me what you will, I will grant it.

Orlando. Then love me, Rosalind.   110

Rosalind. Yes, faith will I, Fridays and Saturdays and all.

Orlando. And wilt thou have me?

Rosalind. Ay, and twenty such.

Orlando. What sayest thou?

Rosalind. Are you not good?

Orlando. I hope so.

Rosalind. Why then, can one desire too much of a good thing? [*she rises*] Come, sister, you shall be the priest and marry us....Give me your hand, Orlando... 120 What do you say, sister?

Orlando. Pray thee, marry us.

Celia. I cannot say the words.

Rosalind. You must begin, 'Will you, Orlando'—

Celia. Go to...Will you, Orlando, have to wife this Rosalind?

Orlando. I will.

Rosalind. Ay, but when?

Orlando. Why now, as fast as she can marry us.

Rosalind. Then you must say, 'I take thee, Rosalind, 130 for wife.'

Orlando. I take thee, Rosalind, for wife.

Rosalind. I might ask you for your commission, but I do take thee, Orlando, for my husband...There's a girl goes before the priest, and certainly a woman's thought runs before her actions.

Orlando. So do all thoughts, they are winged.

Rosalind. Now tell me how long you would have her after you have possessed her.

140 *Orlando.* For ever and a day.

Rosalind. Say 'a day' without the 'ever'...No, no, Orlando, men are April when they woo, December when they wed; maids are May when they are maids, but the sky changes when they are wives...I will be more jealous of thee than a Barbary cock-pigeon over his hen, more clamorous than a parrot against rain, more new-fangled than an ape, more giddy in my desires than a monkey: I will weep for nothing, like Diana in the fountain, and I will do that when you are disposed
150 to be merry; I will laugh like a hyen, and that when thou art inclined to sleep.

Orlando. But will my Rosalind do so?

Rosalind. By my life, she will do as I do.

Orlando. O, but she is wise.

Rosalind. Or else she could not have the wit to do this: the wiser, the waywarder: make the doors upon a woman's wit, and it will out at the casement; shut that, and 'twill out at the key-hole; stop that, 'twill fly with the smoke out at the chimney.

160 *Orlando.* A man that had a wife with such a wit, he might say 'Wit, whither wilt?'

Rosalind. Nay, you might keep that check for it, till you met your wife's wit going to your neighbour's bed.

Orlando. And what wit could wit have to excuse that?

Rosalind. Marry, to say she came to seek you there... You shall never take her without her answer, unless you take her without her tongue: O, that woman that cannot make her fault her husband's occasion, let her
170 never nurse her child herself, for she will breed it like a fool.

Orlando. For these two hours, Rosalind, I will leave thee.

Rosalind. Alas, dear love, I cannot lack thee two hours!

Orlando. I must attend the duke at dinner. By two o'clock I will be with thee again.

Rosalind. Ay, go your ways, go your ways; I knew what you would prove, my friends told me as much, and I thought no less: that flattering tongue of yours won me: 'tis but one cast away, and so, come death.... 180 Two o'clock is your hour?

Orlando. Ay, sweet Rosalind.

Rosalind. By my troth, and in good earnest, and so God mend me, and by all pretty oaths that are not dangerous, if you break one jot of your promise, or come one minute behind your hour, I will think you the most pathetical break-promise, and the most hollow lover, and the most unworthy of her you call Rosalind, that may be chosen out of the gross band of the unfaithful: therefore beware my censure, and keep your 190 promise.

Orlando. With no less religion than if thou wert indeed my Rosalind: so adieu.

Rosalind. Well, Time is the old justice that examines all such offenders, and let Time try: adieu!   [*he goes*

Celia. You have simply misused our sex in your love-prate: we must have your doublet and hose plucked over your head, and show the world what the bird hath done to her own nest.

Rosalind. O coz, coz, coz...my pretty little coz, that 200 thou didst know how many fathom deep I am in love! But it cannot be sounded; my affection hath an unknown bottom, like the bay of Portugal.

Celia. Or rather, bottomless—that as fast as you pour affection in, it runs out.

Rosalind. No, that same wicked bastard of Venus, that was begot of thought, conceived of spleen, and born of madness—that blind rascally boy that abuses every one's eyes because his own are out—let him be judge how 210 deep I am in love…I'll tell thee, Aliena, I cannot be out of the sight of Orlando: I'll go find a shadow and sigh till he come.

Celia. And I'll sleep.   *[they go*

[4. 2.] *Before the cave of the exiled Duke. A noise as of huntsmen approaching. Presently* AMIENS *and other lords appear, dressed as foresters, with* JAQUES *in their midst to whom they are telling of their morning's sport*

Jaques. Which is he that killed the deer?

A lord. Sir, it was I.

Jaques. Let's present him to the duke, like a Roman conqueror. And it would do well to set the deer's horns upon his head, for a branch of victory…Have you no song, forester, for this purpose?

Amiens. Yes, sir.

Jaques. Sing it: 'tis no matter how it be in tune, so it make noise enough.

He that killed the deer is first clad in horns and skin, and then raised aloft by the company, who 'sing him home,' Amiens leading and the rest joining in chorus

The Song

10   What shall he have that killed the deer?
        His leather skin and horns to wear:
        Then sing him home—the rest shall bear
            This burden…
            Take thou no scorn to wear the horn,
            It was a crest ere thou wast born,

> Thy father's father wore it,
> And thy father bore it,
> The horn, the horn, the lusty horn,.
> Is not a thing to laugh to scorn.

*They march thrice around the tree, repeating the burthen
again and again; then they turn into the Duke's cave*

[4. 3.]   *The clearing near the sheepcote*

ROSALIND *and* CELIA *return*

Rosalind. How say you now? Is it not past two
o'clock? and here much Orlando!

Celia. I warrant you, with pure love and troubled
brain, he hath ta'en his bow and arrows, and is gone
forth to sleep...Look, who comes here.

SILVIUS *approaches*

Silvius. My errand is to you, fair youth—
My gentle Phebe bid me give you this:

                            [*he gives Rosalind a letter*

I know not the contents, but as I guess
By the stern brow and waspish action
Which she did use as she was writing of it,   10
It bears an angry tenour: pardon me,
I am but as a guiltless messenger.

Rosalind. Patience herself would startle at this letter,
And play the swaggerer—bear this, bear all:
She says I am not fair, that I lack manners,
She calls me proud, and that she could not love me
Were man as rare as phœnix: 'od's my will!
Her love is not the hare that I do hunt.
Why writes she so to me? Well, shepherd, well,
This is a letter of your own device.   20

Silvius. No, I protest, I know not the contents—
Phebe did write it.

Rosalind.   Come, come, you are a fool,
And turned into the extremity of love.
I saw her hand—she has a leathern hand,
A freestone-coloured hand: I verily did think
That her old gloves were on, but 'twas her hands:
She has a huswife's hand—but that's no matter:
I say she never did invent this letter,
This is a man's invention, and his hand.

30 *Silvius.* Sure, it is hers.
  Rosalind. Why, 'tis a boisterous and a cruel style,
A style for challengers; why, she defies me,
Like Turk to Christian: women's gentle brain
Could not drop forth such giant-rude invention,
Such Ethiop words, blacker in their effect
Than in their countenance...Will you hear the letter?
  Silvius. So please you, for I never heard it yet;
Yet heard too much of Phebe's cruelty.
  Rosalind. She Phebes me: mark how the tyrant writes.

40 [*reads*]   'Art thou god to shepherd turned,
                That a maiden's heart hath burned?'
Can a woman rail thus?
  Silvius. Call you this railing?
  Rosalind. 'Why, thy godhead laid apart,
                Warr'st thou with a woman's heart?'
Did you ever hear such railing?
                'Whiles the eye of man did woo me,
                That could do no vengeance to me.'
Meaning me a beast.

50   'If the scorn of your bright eyne
                Have power to raise such love in mine,
                Alack, in me what strange effect
                Would they work in mild aspéct?
                Whiles you chid me I did love.
                How then might your prayers move?'

He that brings this love to thee
Little knows this love in me:
And by him seal up thy mind,
Whether that thy youth and kind
Will the faithful offer take 60
Of me and all that I can make,
Or else by him my love deny,
And then I'll study how to die.'

Silvius. Call you this chiding?

Celia. Alas, poor shepherd!

Rosalind. Do you pity him? no, he deserves no pity...
Wilt thou love such a woman? What, to make thee an
instrument and play false strains upon thee! not to be
endured! Well, go your way to her (for I see love hath
made thee a tame snake) and say this to her: that if she 70
love me, I charge her to love thee: if she will not, I will
never have her, unless thou entreat for her....If you be
a true lover, hence, and not a word; for here comes more
company. *[he goes*

OLIVER comes up hastily by another path

Oliver. Good morrow, fair ones: pray you, if
you know,
Where in the purlieus of this forest stands
A sheepcote fenced about with olive-trees?

Celia. West of this place, down in the
neighbour bottom—
The rank of osiers by the murmuring stream
Left on your right hand brings you to the place 80
But at this hour the house doth keep itself,
There's none within.

Oliver. If that an eye may profit by a tongue,
Then should I know you by description—
Such garments and such years: 'The boy is fair,

Of female favour, and bestows himself
†Like a ripe forester: the woman low,
And browner than her brother.'…Are not you
The owner of the house I did inquire for?

90   *Celia.* It is no boast, being asked, to say we are.
    Oliver. Orlando doth commend him to you both,
And to that youth he calls his Rosalind
He sends this bloody napkin; are you he?
    Rosalind. I am: what must we understand by this?
    Oliver. Some of my shame, if you will know of me
What man I am, and how, and why, and where
This handkercher was stained.
    Celia.   I pray you, tell it.
    Oliver. When last the young Orlando parted from you
He left a promise to return again

100 Within an hour, and pacing through the forest,
Chewing the food of sweet and bitter fancy,
Lo, what befel! he threw his eye aside,
And mark what object did present itself!
Under an oak, whose boughs were mossed with age
And high top bald with dry antiquity,
A wretched ragged man, o'ergrown with hair,
Lay sleeping on his back: about his neck
A green and gilded snake had wreathed itself,
Who with her head nimble in threats approached

110 The opening of his mouth; but suddenly
Seeing Orlando, it unlinked itself,
And with indented glides did slip away
Into a bush: under which bush's-shade
A lioness, with udders all drawn dry,
Lay couching, head on ground, with catlike watch,
When that the sleeping man should stir; for 'tis
The royal disposition of that beast
To prey on nothing that doth seem as dead:

This seen, Orlando did approach the man,
And found it was his brother, his elder brother. 120

Celia. O, I have heard him speak of that same brother,
And he did render him the most unnatural
That lived 'mongst men.

Oliver. And well he might so do,
For well I know he was unnatural.

Rosalind. But, to Orlando: did he leave him there,
Food to the sucked and hungry lioness?

Oliver. Twice did he turn his back and purposed so:
But kindness, nobler ever than revenge,
And nature, stronger than his just occasion,
Made him give battle to the lioness, 130
Who quickly fell before him: in which hurtling
From miserable slumber I awaked.

Celia. Are you his brother?

Rosalind. Was't you he rescued?

Celia. Was't you that did so oft contrive to kill him?

Oliver. 'Twas I; but 'tis not I: I do not shame
To tell you what I was, since my conversion
So sweetly tastes, being the thing I am.

Rosalind. But, for the bloody napkin?—

Oliver. By and by...
When from the first to last betwixt us two
Tears our recountments had most kindly bathed, 140
As how I came into that desert place....
In brief, he led me to the gentle duke,
Who gave me fresh array and entertainment,
Committing me unto my brother's love,
Who led me instantly unto his cave,
There stripped himself, and here upon his arm
The lioness had torn some flesh away,
Which all this while had bled; and now he fainted,
And cried, in fainting, upon Rosalind....

150 Brief, I recovered him, bound up his wound,
And after some small space being strong at heart,
He sent me hither, stranger as I am,
To tell this story, that you might excuse
His broken promise, and to give this napkin,
Dyed in his blood, unto the shepherd youth
That he in sport doth call his Rosalind.

                              [*Rosalind faints*

    Celia. Why, how now, Ganymede! sweet Gany-
      mede!
    Oliver. Many will swoon when they do look on blood.
    Celia. There is more in it...Cousin, Ganymede!
160   *Oliver.* Look, he recovers.
    Rosalind.   I would I were at home.
    Celia. We'll lead you thither...
I pray you, will you take him by the arm?
    Oliver. Be of good cheer, youth: you a man!
You lack a man's heart.
    Rosalind.   I do so, I confess it...
Ah, sirrah, a body would think this was well counter-
feited. I pray you, tell your brother how well I
counterfeited....Heigh-ho!
    Oliver. This was not counterfeit, there is too great
testimony in your complexion that it was a passion of
170 earnest.
    Rosalind. Counterfeit, I assure you.
    Oliver. Well then, take a good heart, and counterfeit
to be a man.
    Rosalind. So I do: but, i'faith, I should have been a
woman by right.
    Celia. Come, you look paler and paler; pray you,
draw homewards...Good sir, go with us.
    Oliver. That will I: for I must bear answer back
How you excuse my brother, Rosalind.

Rosalind. I shall devise something: but, I pray you commend my counterfeiting to him...Will you go?

[*they descend towards the cottage*

[5.1.] TOUCHSTONE *and* AUDREY *come through the trees*

Touchstone. We shall find a time, Audrey—patience, gentle Audrey.

Audrey. Faith, the priest was good enough, for all th old gentleman's saying.

Touchstone. A most wicked Sir Oliver, Audrey, a most vile Martext....But, Audrey, there is a youth here in the forest lays claim to you.

Audrey. Ay, I know who 'tis; he hath no interest in me in the world: here comes the man you mean.

WILLIAM *enters the clearing*

Touchstone. It is meat and drink to me to see a clown. 10 By my troth, we that have good wits have much to answer for; we shall be flouting; we cannot hold.

William. Good ev'n, Audrey.

Audrey. God ye good ev'n, William.

William. And good ev'n to you, sir.

Touchstone [*with mock-dignity*]. Good ev'n, gentle friend. Cover thy head, cover thy head; nay, prithee, be covered....How old are you, friend?

William. Five-and-twenty, sir.

Touchstone. A ripe age...Is thy name, William? 20

William. William, sir.

Touchstone. A fair name...Wast born i'th' forest here?

William. Ay sir, I thank God.

Touchstone. 'Thank God'; a good answer...Art rich?

William. Faith sir, so so.

Touchstone. 'So so' is good, very good, very excellent good: and yet it is not, it is but so so...Art thou wise?

30 *William.* Ay sir, I have a pretty wit.

Touchstone. Why, thou say'st well....I do now remember a saying: 'The fool doth think he is wise, but the wise man knows himself to be a fool'...[*By this William's mouth is wide open with amazement*] The heathen philosopher, when he had a desire to eat a grape, would open his lips when he put it into his mouth, meaning thereby that grapes were made to eat and lips to open....You do love this maid?

William. I do, sir.

40 *Touchstone.* Give me your hand...Art thou learned?

William. No, sir.

Touchstone. Then learn this of me—to have, is to have; for it is a figure in rhetoric that drink, being poured out of a cup into a glass, by filling the one doth empty the other; for all your writers do consent that ipse is he: now, you are not ipse, for I am he.

William. Which he, sir?

Touchstone. He, sir, that must marry this woman... Therefore, you clown, abandon (which is in the vulgar

50 'leave') the society (which in the boorish is 'company') of this female (which in the common is 'woman'); which together is, 'abandon the society of this female,' or, clown, thou perishest; or, to thy better understanding, diest; or, to wit, I kill thee, make thee away, translate thy life into death, thy liberty into bondage: I will deal in poison with thee, or in bastinado, or in steel; I will bandy with thee in faction; I will o'er-run thee with policy; I will kill thee a hundred and fifty ways—therefore tremble and depart.

60 *Audrey.* Do, good William.

William. God rest you merry, sir.   [*he goes*

Corin appears and calls

Corin. Our master and mistress seek you : come, away, away.

Touchstone. Trip, Audrey, trip, Audrey—I attend, I attend.   [*they run off towards the cottage*

A night passes

[5.2.]   OLIVER *and* ORLANDO (*his arm in a scarf*) *seated on a bank*

Orlando. Is't possible that on so little acquaintance you should like her? that but seeing you should love her? and loving woo? and, wooing, she should grant? and will you persever to enjoy her?

Oliver. Neither call the giddiness of it in question, the poverty of her, the small acquaintance, my sudden wooing, nor her sudden consenting; but say with me, I love Aliena; say with her that she loves me; consent with both that we may enjoy each other: it shall be to your good; for my father's house and all the revenue   10
that was old Sir Rowland's will I estate upon you, and here live and die a shepherd.

ROSALIND is seen coming in the distance

Orlando. You have my consent....Let your wedding be to-morrow: thither will I invite the duke and all's contented followers...Go you and prepare Aliena; for look you, here comes my Rosalind.

Rosalind. God save you, brother.

Oliver. And you, fair sister.   [*he goes*

Rosalind. O, my dear Orlando, how it grieves me to see thee wear thy heart in a scarf.   20

Orlando. It is my arm.

Rosalind. I thought thy heart had been wounded with the claws of a lion.

Orlando. Wounded it is, but with the eyes of a lady.

Rosalind. Did your brother tell you how I counter-feited to swoon, when he showed me your handkercher?

Orlando. Ay, and greater wonders than that.

Rosalind. O, I know where you are: nay, 'tis true: there was never any thing so sudden but the fight of
30 two rams, and Cæsar's thrasonical brag of 'I came, saw, and overcame': for your brother and my sister no sooner met but they looked; no sooner looked but they loved; no sooner loved but they sighed; no sooner sighed but they asked one another the reason; no sooner knew the reason but they sought the remedy: and in these degrees have they made a pair of stairs to marriage, which they will climb incontinent, or else be incontinent before marriage: they are in the very wrath of love, and they will together; clubs cannot part them.

40 *Orlando.* They shall be married to-morrow; and I will bid the duke to the nuptial....But, O, how bitter a thing it is to look into happiness through another man's eyes! By so much the more shall I to-morrow be at the height of heart-heaviness, by how much I shall think my brother happy in having what he wishes for.

Rosalind. Why then, to-morrow I cannot serve your turn for Rosalind?

Orlando. I can live no longer by thinking.

Rosalind. I will weary you then no longer with idle
50 talking....Know of me then, for now I speak to some purpose, that I know you are a gentleman of good conceit: I speak not this that you should bear a good opinion of my knowledge, insomuch I say I know you are; neither do I labour for a greater esteem than may in some little measure draw a belief from you, to do your-self good and not to grace me....Believe then, if you please, that I can do strange things: I have, since I was

three year old, conversed with a magician, most profound in his art, and yet not damnable....If you do love
Rosalind so near the heart as your gesture cries it out, 60
when your brother marries Aliena, shall you marry her.
I know into what straits of fortune she is driven, and
it is not impossible to me, if it appear not inconvenient
to you, to set her before your eyes to-morrow, human
as she is, and without any danger.

Orlando. Speak'st thou in sober meanings?

Rosalind. By my life I do, which I tender dearly,
though I say I am a magician...Therefore, put you in
your best array, bid your friends; for if you will be
married to-morrow, you shall; and to Rosalind, if you 70
will.

SILVIUS and PHEBE draw near

Look, here comes a lover of mine and a lover of hers.

Phebe. Youth, you have done me much ungentleness,
To show the letter that I writ to you.

Rosalind. I care not if I have: it is my study
To seem despiteful and ungentle to you:
You are there followed by a faithful shepherd—
Look upon him, love him; he worships you.

Phebe. Good shepherd, tell this youth what 'tis to
    love.

Silvius. It is to be all made of sighs and tears,   80
And so am I for Phebe.

Phebe. And I for Ganymede.

Orlando. And I for Rosalind.

Rosalind. And I for no woman.

Silvius. It is to be all made of faith and service,
And so am I for Phebe.

Phebe. And I for Ganymede.

Orlando. And I for Rosalind.

Rosalind. And I for no woman.

90 *Silvius.* It is to be all made of fantasy,
All made of passion, and all made of wishes,
All adoration, duty and observance,
All humbleness, all patience, and impatience,
All purity, all trial, all obedience;
And so am I for Phebe.
    Phebe. And so am I for Ganymede.
    Orlando. And so am I for Rosalind.
    Rosalind. And so am I for no woman.
    Phebe [*to Rosalind*]. If this be so, why blame you me
    to love you?
100 *Silvius* [*to Phebe*]. If this be so, why blame you me
    to love you?
    Orlando. If this be so, why blame you me to love you?
    Rosalind. Who do you speak to, 'Why blame you me
    to love you?'
    Orlando. To her that is not here, nor doth not hear.
    Rosalind. Pray you no more of this, 'tis like the howling
of Irish wolves against the Moon...[*to Silvius*] I will
help you, if I can...[*to Phebe*] I would love you, if I
could...To-morrow meet me all together...[*to Phebe*]
I will marry you, if ever I marry woman, and I'll be
married to-morrow...[*to Orlando*] I will satisfy you, if
110 ever I satisfied man, and you shall be married to-
morrow...[*to Silvius*] I will content you, if what
pleases you contents you, and you shall be married to-
morrow...[*to Orlando*] As you love Rosalind, meet.
[*to Silvius*] As you love Phebe, meet. And as I love
no woman, I'll meet....So, fare you well; I have left
you commands.
    Silvius. I'll not fail, if I live.
    Phebe. Nor I.
    Orlando. Nor I.   [*they disperse*

[5. 3.]   *TOUCHSTONE and AUDREY enter the clearing*

Touchstone. To-morrow is the joyful day, Audrey. To-morrow will we be married.

Audrey. I do desire it with all my heart: and I hope it is no dishonest desire to desire to be a woman of the world. Here come two of the banished duke's pages.

Two pages run up

First Page. Well met, honest gentleman.

Touchstone. By my troth, well met...Come, sit, sit, and a song.

Second Page. We are for you: sit i'th' middle.

First Page. Shall we clap into't roundly, without 10 hawking or spitting or saying we are hoarse, which are the only prologues to a bad voice?

Second Page. I'faith i'faith; and both in a tune, like two gipsies on a horse.

Song

It was a lover and his lass,
     With a hey, and a ho, and a hey nonino:
That o'er the green corn-field did pass,
     In spring time, the only pretty ring time,
When birds do sing, hey ding a ding, ding,
Sweet lovers love the spring.   20

Between the acres of the rye,
     With a hey, and a ho, and a hey nonino:
These pretty country folks would lie,
     In spring time, the only pretty ring time,
When birds do sing, hey ding a ding, ding,
Sweet lovers love the spring.

This carol they began that hour,
     With a hey, and a ho, and a hey nonino:
How that life was but a flower,

30   In spring time, the only pretty ring time,
             When birds do sing, hey ding a ding, ding,
             Sweet lovers love the spring.

        And therefore take the present time,
             With a hey, and a ho, and a hey nonino:
        For love is crownéd with the prime,
             In spring time, the only pretty ring time,
             When birds do sing, hey ding a ding, ding,
             Sweet lovers love the spring.

Touchstone. Truly, young gentlemen, though there was
40 no great matter in the ditty, yet the note was very untuneable.

First Page. You are deceived, sir—we kept time, we
lost not our time.

Touchstone. By my troth, yes; I count it but time lost
to hear such a foolish song....God buy you, and God
mend your voices! Come, Audrey.   [*they go*

A night passes

[5. 4.]   *The clearing near the sheepcote (as before)*

The exiled DUKE, AMIENS, JAQUES, ORLANDO,
OLIVER, and CELIA

Duke. Dost thou believe, Orlando, that the boy
Can do all this that he hath promiséd?

Orlando. I sometimes do believe, and sometimes do not,
As those that fear they hope, and know they fear.

ROSALIND, SILVIUS, and PHEBE join the company

Rosalind. Patience once more, whiles our compáct
    is urged:
You say, if I bring in your Rosalind,
You will bestow her on Orlando here?

Duke. That would I, had I kingdoms to give
   with her.

Rosalind. And you say you will have her, when I
   bring her?

Orlando. That would I, were I of all kingdoms king. 10

Rosalind. You say you'll marry me, if I be willing?

Phebe. That will I, should I die the hour after.

Rosalind. But if you do refuse to marry me,
You'll give yourself to this most faithful shepherd?

Phebe. So is the bargain.

Rosalind. You say that you'll have Phebe, if she
   will?

Silvius. Though to have her and death were both
   one thing.

Rosalind. I have promised to make all this matter
   even...

Keep you your word, O duke, to give your daughter—
You yours, Orlando, to receive his daughter: 20
Keep your word, Phebe, that you'll marry me,
Or else refusing me, to wed this shepherd:
Keep your word, Silvius, that you'll marry her,
If she refuse me—and from hence I go,
To make these doubts all even.

        [*she beckons to Celia and they depart together*

Duke. I do remember in this shepherd-boy
Some lively touches of my daughter's favour.

  Orlando. My lord, the first time that I ever saw
   him,
Methought he was a brother to your daughter:
But, my good lord, this boy is forest-born,   30
And hath been tutored in the rudiments
Of many desperate studies by his uncle,
Whom he reports to be a great magician,
Obscuréd in the circle of this forest.

Touchstone and Audrey enter the clearing

Jaques. There is, sure, another flood toward, and these couples are coming to the ark. Here comes a pair of very strange beasts, which in all tongues are called fools.

Touchstone. Salutation and greeting to you all!

Jaques. Good my lord, bid him welcome: this is the
40 motley-minded gentleman that I have so often met in the forest: he hath been a courtier, he swears.

Touchstone. If any man doubt that, let him put me to my purgation. I have trod a measure—I have flattered a lady—I have been politic with my friend, smooth with mine enemy—I have undone three tailors—I have had four quarrels, and like to have fought one.

Jaques. And how was that ta'en up?

Touchstone. Faith, we met, and found the quarrel was upon the seventh cause.

50 *Jaques.* How seventh cause? Good my lord, like this fellow.

Duke. I like him very well.

Touchstone. God'ild you, sir, I desire you of the like... I press in here, sir, amongst the rest of the country copulatives, to swear and to forswear, according as marriage binds and blood breaks...[*he waves towards Audrey*] A poor virgin, sir, an ill-favoured thing, sir, but mine own—a poor humour of mine, sir, to take that that no man else will: rich honesty dwells like a
60 miser, sir, in a poor house, as your pearl in your foul oyster.

Duke. By my faith, he is very swift and sententious.

Touchstone. According to the fool's bolt, sir, and such dulcet diseases.

Jaques. But, for the seventh cause. How did you find the quarrel on the seventh cause?

Touchstone. Upon a lie seven times removed...bear your body more seeming, Audrey...as thus, sir: I did dislike the cut of a certain courtier's beard: he sent me word, if I said his beard was not cut well, he was in the mind it was: this is called the Retort Courteous. If I sent him word again 'it was not well cut,' he would send me word, he cut it to please himself: this is called the Quip Modest. If again 'it was not well cut,' he disabled my judgement: this is called the Reply Churlish. If again 'it was not well cut,' he would answer, I spake not true: this is called the Reproof Valiant. If again 'it was not well cut,' he would say, I lie: this is called the Countercheck Quarrelsome: and so to the Lie Circumstantial and the Lie Direct.

Jaques. And how oft did you say his beard was not well cut?

Touchstone. I durst go no further than the Lie Circumstantial: nor he durst not give me the Lie Direct: and so we measured swords and parted.

Jaques. Can you nominate in order now the degrees of the lie?

Touchstone. O sir, we quarrel in print—by the book: as you have books for good manners...I will name you the degrees. The first, the Retort Courteous; the second, the Quip Modest; the third, the Reply Churlish; the fourth, the Reproof Valiant; the fifth, the Countercheck Quarrelsome; the sixth, the Lie with Circumstance; the seventh, the Lie Direct...All these you may avoid, but the Lie Direct; and you may avoid that too, with an If. I knew when seven justices could not take up a quarrel, but when the parties were met themselves, one of them thought but of an If; as, 'If you said so, then I said so': and they shook hands and swore brothers. Your If is the only peace-maker; much virtue in If.

Jaques. Is not this a rare fellow, my lord? he's as good at any thing, and yet a fool!

Duke. He uses his folly like a stalking-horse, and under the presentation of that he shoots his wit.

Enter, as in a masque, persons representing Hymen and his train, together with Rosalind and Celia in their proper habits. 'Still music'

Hymen sings

> Then is there mirth in heaven,
> When earthly things made even
>   Atone together.
> Good duke, receive thy daughter,
> Hymen from heaven brought her,
>   Yea, brought her hither,
> That thou mightst join her hand with his
> Whose heart within her bosom is.

Rosalind [*to the Duke*]. To you I give myself, for I
    am yours.

[*to Orlando*] To you I give myself, for I am yours.

Duke. If there be truth in sight, you are my daughter.

Orlando. If there be truth in sight, you are my
    Rosalind.

Phebe. If sight and shape be true,
Why then, my love adieu!

Rosalind. I'll have no father, if you be not he:
I'll have no husband, if you be not he:
Nor ne'er wed woman, if you be not she.

Hymen. Peace, ho! I bar confusion.
    'Tis I must make conclusion
        Of these most strange events:
    Here's eight that must take hands,
    To join in Hymen's bands,
        If truth holds true contents.

You and you no cross shall part:
You and you are heart in heart:
You to his love must accord,   130
Or have a woman to your lord.
You and you are sure together,
As the winter to foul weather.
Whiles a wedlock-hymn we sing,
Feed yourselves with questioning;
That reason wonder may diminish,
How thus we met, and these things finish.

Choric song
Wedding is great Juno's crown,
   O blesséd bond of board and bed:
'Tis Hymen peoples every town,   140
   High wedlock then be honouréd:
Honour, high honour and renown,
To Hymen, god of every town!

Duke. O my dear niece, welcome thou art to me,
Even daughter, welcome, in no less degree.

Phebe [*to Silvius*]. I will not eat my word, now
   thou art mine,
Thy faith my fancy to thee doth combine.

Enter JAQUES DE BOYS

Jaques de Boys. Let me have audience for a word
   or two:
I am the second son of old Sir Rowland,
That bring these tidings to this fair assembly.   150
Duke Frederick, hearing how that every day
Men of great worth resorted to this forest,
Addressed a mighty power, which were on foot,
In his own conduct, purposely to take
His brother here and put him to the sword:
And to the skirts of this wild wood he came;

Where, meeting with an old religious man,
After some question with him, was converted
Both from his enterprise and from the world:
160 His crown bequeathing to his banished brother,
And all their lands restored to them again
That were with him exiled...This to be true,
I do engage my life.
  Duke.   Welcome, young man;
Thou offer'st fairly to thy brothers' wedding:
To one his lands withheld, and to the other
A land itself at large, a potent dukedom.
First, in this forest, let us do those ends
That here were well begun and well begot:
And after, every of this happy number,
170 That have endured shrewd days and nights with us,
Shall share the good of our returnéd fortune,
According to the measure of their states.
Meantime, forget this new-fall'n dignity,
And fall into our rustic revelry...
Play, music! and you brides and bridegrooms all,
With measure heaped in joy, to th' measures fall.
  Jaques. Sir, by your patience... [*he stays the music*
[*to Jaques de Boys*]   If I heard you rightly,
The duke hath put on a religious life,
And thrown into neglect the pompous court?
180 *Jaques de Boys*. He hath.
  Jaques. To him will I: out of these convertites
There is much matter to be heard and learned....
[*to the Duke*] You to your former honour I bequeath,
Your patience and your virtue well deserves it:
[*to Orlando*] You to a love, that your true faith doth
   merit:
[*to Oliver*] You to your land, and love, and great allies:
[*to Silvius*] You to a long and well-deservéd bed:

[*to Touchstone*] And you to wrangling, for thy
　　　loving voyage
Is but for two months victualled...So to your pleasures,
I am for other than for dancing measures.　　190
　Duke. Stay, Jaques, stay.
　Jaques. To see no pastime, I: what you would have
I'll stay to know at your abandoned cave.
　　　　　　　　　　　　　[*he turns from them*
　Duke. Proceed, proceed: we will begin these rites,
As we do trust they'll end in true delights.
　　　　　　　Music and dance

Epilogue

spoken by Rosalind

It is not the fashion to see the lady the epilogue: but
it is no more unhandsome than to see the lord the
prologue. If it be true that good wine needs no bush,
'tis true that a good play needs no epilogue: yet to good
wine they do use good bushes; and good plays prove
the better by the help of good epilogues...What a case
am I in then, that am neither a good epilogue nor
cannot insinuate with you in the behalf of a good play!
I am not furnished like a beggar, therefore to beg will
10 not become me: my way is to conjure you, and I'll
begin with the women. I charge you, O women, for
the love you bear to men, to like as much of this play
as please you: and I charge you, O men, for the love
you bear to women—as I perceive by your simpering,
none of you hates them—that between you and the
women the play may please. If I were a woman, I
would kiss as many of you as had beards that pleased
me, complexions that liked me, and breaths that I defied
not: and, I am sure, as many as have good beards, or
20 good faces, or sweet breaths, will, for my kind offer,
when I make curtsy, bid me farewell.

THE COPY FOR
AS YOU LIKE IT, 1623

The First Folio is our sole authority for the text of
As You Like It; and as the copy for the play was entered
to Blount and Jaggard in the Stationers' Register on
8 November 1623, together with such of the rest of
'Mr. William Shakspeers Comedyes, Histories and
Tragedyes...as are not formerly entred to other men,'
it is pretty certain that it had not previously appeared in
print. Another entry in the Register suggests, however,
that it narrowly escaped being printed twenty-three
years earlier. The entry in question is the famous note
of 4 August 1600, directing four plays belonging to the
Lord Chamberlain's Men 'to be staied'; the four being
As You Like It, Henry V, Every Man in his Humour,
and *Much Ado*. This staying order, which Dr A. W.
Pollard interprets as a precaution by Shakespeare's
Company against an anticipated piracy[1], was frustrated
as far as *Henry V* was concerned, seeing that a pirated
text of this play was issued in 1600, though whether
before or after the order is unknown, and was of merely
temporary service as regards *Much Ado* and *Every Man
in his Humour*, which were also published in the same
year, though after due entry in the Register and doubtless with the full consent of the company to which they
belonged. But with *As You Like It* the order was both
effective and absolute. From this it may reasonably be
inferred that *As You Like It* was a popular play with
London theatre-goers in 1600. That the pirates were
after them shows that all four plays had won sufficient
renown on the stage to be worth stealing; that the
players were, on the other hand, willing to release the

[1] *Shakespeare Folios and Quartos*, p. 67.

manuscripts of *Much Ado* and *Every Man in his Humour* and not of *As You Like It* suggests that while the stage-popularity of the two first-mentioned was on the ebb, that of the latter was still at the flood[1]. This entry of 1600 is, therefore, a valuable piece of evidence as to the date of the play's composition; it is indeed the only evidence of an external kind that we possess.

I. *Revision-clues*

As You Like It then was in existence, and probably being played to enthusiastic audiences, in the year 1600. Had it any textual history before or after this date? It was not printed until 1623, and much might happen to prompt-copy in twenty-three years at the theatre. Or to look in the other direction, the popular play of 1600 need not necessarily have been a new play; it may like *Hamlet* have been an old one rehandled. One thing at least is certain: history of a kind lies behind the transmitted text, since it is evident that some of the scenes now in prose had once been in blank verse. The textual editor owes the discovery of this fact to Dr A. W. Pollard, who when making a study of *As You Like It* some years ago, came to the conclusion that the prose-lines with which 5. 2. opens had originally been verse, and communicated his conclusion in a private letter[2]. The verse-fossils are only to be found in the first eighteen lines of the scene, ten of which, if two small words be omitted, form a continuous passage which even the most sceptical or the most conservative of critics must admit to be verse. Thus ll. 8–18 run:

> Consent with both that we [may] enjoy each other:
> It shall be to your good; [for] my father's house

[1] Cf. *Ado*, p. 102.
[2] Similar evidence for textual revision has already been noted in *Temp.* (p. 79), *Two Gent.* (p. 80), *Meas.* (p. 108), while Prof. A. E. Morgan has made notable use of it in *Some Problems of Shakespeare's 'Henry IV'* (Shak. Assoc.), 1924.

And all the revenue that was old Sir Rowland's
Will I estate upon you, and here live
And die a shepherd.
    Orl.   You have my consent....
Let your wedding be to-morrow: thither will I
Invite the duke and all's contented followers:
Go you and prepare Aliena; for look you,
Here comes my Rosalind.
    Ros.   God save you, brother.
    Oli. And you, fair sister.   [*exit Oliver*

And lest any one should pretend that this is mere accident, that Shakespeare's prose had a rhythm of its own which here for a few lines happens to coincide with the rhythm of blank verse, the Folio offers confirmation that Shakespeare was at least consciously composing verse when he penned the speech of Orlando given above, seeing that it prints it as verse. On the other hand, it is equally certain that Shakespeare intended the whole episode to be taken as prose, inasmuch as the opening of the scene, though genuine prose enough, contains several lines which with a little alteration become verse. Here are some:

Is't possible that on so *slight* acquaintance

But seeing you should love [her]? and loving woo?
And wooing she should grant? [and] will you perséver

My sudden wooing nor her *quick* consenting;
But say with me, I love *my* Aliena.

There is really no escaping the facts. The first eighteen lines of 5. 2., down to the exit of Oliver, were originally verse and were re-written as prose before the play took its final form. It should be noticed that the only portion of the scene thus affected are the lines concerned with Oliver, for there is no trace of verse in the dialogue between Rosalind and Orlando that follows; which suggests that the revision affected certain elements in the plot more than others.

'But is there anything more in all this,' our sceptic

may enquire, 'than a change of mind on the part of Shakespeare? He began to write the scene in verse, thought better of it, and made a fresh start in prose, using a few scraps of his first draft when he found them convenient. It all might have happened in a single afternoon.' Not quite, we think; for the discovery of verse-fossils in the prose of 5. 2. naturally led to a search for the same thing elsewhere, and though some of the prose-scenes of the play are, like ll. 19–71 of 5. 2., innocent of all traces of verse, and in others the traces are but faint, there can be no doubt about their presence in the prose-scenes, or the prose-sections, of 1. 2., 2. 6. and 4. 3.[1] But a 'change of mind' which leads to the re-writing of four scenes scattered evenly throughout the play is more than a passing whim, and involves more than an afternoon's work. It amounts to something like a revision of the play as a whole. Such a revision might, of course, still be an incident, so to speak, in the original composition of the play. Shakespeare, for instance, may have written a number of scenes or episodes in verse, when preparing his first draft, and then in making out his text for the acting company have re-written the verse for some reason as he went through the manuscript. Apart from the fact that we do not believe that Shakespeare, whose 'mind and hand went together,' to whom composition came so easy that his fellow-players boasted that 'he never blotted a line,' and who was above all things economical both of energy and material, would be in the least likely to work in this fashion, there is other evidence in favour of the revision which goes to show that the time which elapsed between the first and the second draft must have been long enough for changes in the cast to have intervened and for Shakespeare to have forgotten some material points in the plot.

[1] The reader is referred to the notes for the evidence in respect of 2. 6. and 4. 3.

It will be convenient, and we think illuminating, to consider this evidence in connexion with the signs of revision in I. 2., which we noted above as a scene particularly rich in verse-fossils. The scene is a long one and once more it is significant that the fossil lines of verse are to be found in one section only of it, viz. that which concerns the wrestling-match (ll. 139–209). But let us first consider the relics of verse, some of which, as the italics and square brackets testify, we have recovered by a little innocent faking.

How now, daughter and cousin, are you crept
Hither to see the wrestling?/Ay, my liege,
So please you give us leave.

Speak to him, ladies; see if you can move him.

Monsieur the challenger, the princess calls for you.
I *do* attend them with all respect and duty.

No, fair princess: he is the general challenger.
I come but in, as others do, to try...

Young gentleman, your spirits are too bold...
You have seen cruel proof of this man's strength.

Your reputation shall not [therefore] be misprized
                    ...go with me to my trial:
Wherein if I be foiled, there is but one shamed...

My friends no wrong, for I have none to *mourn* me,
The world no injury, for in it I have nothing:
Only *i'th'* world *do* I fill up a place...
Better supplied when I have made it empty.

Where's this young gallant that is so desirous
To lie with his mother earth?
                    Ready, sir;
[but] His will hath in it a more modest working

Beseech your grace—I am not yet well breathed.
How dost thou, Charles?
                    He cannot speak, my lord.
Bear him away...What is thy name, young man?

After which the episode closes, appropriately enough, with a speech from the Duke in verse and duly printed as such in the Folio.

This wrestling episode, with its verse-fossils, forms a kind of link between the 138 lines of prose, without a trace of verse, at the opening of the scene, and the sixty-six lines of unmixed verse with which the scene ends. Now it seems natural to suppose that this transition from prose to verse has something to do with the revision of the scene; in other words, that Shakespeare began revising the scene in prose and in a pretty drastic manner, but found himself as he proceeded with his task able to retain more and more of the original matter, leaving the last 66 lines entirely unaltered. On this hypothesis the scene falls into three sections: (i) new prose, ll. 1–138; (ii) old verse re-written as prose, ll. 139–211; and (iii) old verse, ll. 212–277.

Let us turn now to certain inconsistencies in the play, and particularly in this scene, and see if they throw any light upon the question of revision. We may begin with one that has pulled up short every editor of the text. There are, as all the world knows, two dukes in *As You Like It*: the usurper and his banished brother. The pair are distinguished in the speech-headings of the Folio as *Duke* and *Duke Senior*, and no doubt the labels were adequate enough for stage-purposes. But when the modern editor, with his list of *dramatis personae* to make out, seeks for names, the search proves fruitless as far as the elder brother is concerned, while it is only at the very end of the play (5. 4. 151) that the younger is directly spoken of as 'Duke Frederick,' though in the light of this evidence it becomes clear that the 'Frederick' to whom Orlando refers at 1. 2. 222 is the usurper. Both these references, be it noted, occur in verse-passages, and the second in particular belongs to what we have just claimed as the unrevised portion of 1. 2. Now except at these two places the name Frederick is to be found only once elsewhere in the play, this time in the prose-section with which 1. 2. opens and in a context which points unmistakably to the other duke! As the

point is obscured in modern texts by editorial emendation, it is as well to have the words of the Folio before
us (ll. 75–9). They follow Touchstone's discourse of
the Knight, the Pancakes and the Mustard:

Cel. Prethee, who is't that thou means't?

Clo. One that old Fredericke your Father loues.

Rof. My Fathers loue is enough to honor him enough;
fpeake no more of him, you'l be whipt for taxation one of
thefe daies.

Because 'Frederick was not her father but Celia's,'
Theobald deprived Rosalind of her speech and gave it
to her cousin, and all modern editors follow him.
Nevertheless, the Folio assignment is undoubtedly
correct. Capell long ago pointed out that the epithet
'old' clearly belongs to Duke Senior, and that 'we have
no cause to think that Celia would have been so alert
in taking up the clown for reflecting upon her father.'
Apart from this the injured pride in the words 'My
father's love is enough to honour him' and the con-
tingent threat in 'you'll be whipped for taxation one of
these days' must belong to Rosalind, while it is hardly
credible that even a licensed fool would dare to refer to
the duke *de facto*—and so irascible a tyrant!—as 'old
Frederick.' This being so we are forced to conclude
that 'old Frederick' was a mistake on the part of Shakespeare, who in revising the play remembered the name
Frederick but forgot that it belonged to the younger and
not the older duke. And that the name should be used
incorrectly at 1. 2. 76 and correctly at 1. 2. 222 supplies
a pretty piece of evidence in support of our textual
analysis of that scene.

Other inconsistencies can be most readily explained
in the same fashion. There is, for instance, a glaring
inconsistency as regards time, as was first pointed out,
we believe, by P. A. Daniel[1]. In the opening scene of

---

[1] *Time-analysis of the plots of Shakespeare's plays* (New
Shak. Soc.), p. 156.

the play, a prose-scene we may note in passing, Oliver and Charles inform us in conversation that the political events which placed the usurper Frederick on the throne and drove his elder brother into banishment, had taken place quite recently. Daniel notes that 'nothing new at Court has occurred since' the banishment, that Oliver's question, 'Where will the old duke live?', and Charles's reply 'They say he is already in the forest of Arden' imply that what Oliver calls 'the new court' is very new indeed, and that so lately had the old duke been deposed that it was only a man just come from court, like Charles, the usurper's favourite wrestler, who could tell whether Rosalind had been exiled with her father or not. When we turn, however, to 1. 3., which we observe is mainly in verse, it appears that the old duke's banishment had occurred years before; for this is the only possible inter-pretation of the following passage between Duke Frederick and Celia, where the latter pleads for Rosa-lind (ll. 67–72):

> *Duke F.* Ay, Celia, we stayed her for your sake,
> Else had she with her father ranged along.
> *Celia.* I did not then entreat to have her stay,
> It was your pleasure and your own remorse.
> I was too young that time to value her,
> But now I know her.

Furthermore, in 2. 1., another verse-scene, we get the strong impression that the duke and his co-mates in exile had been long resident in Arden, an impression which can hardly be illusory in view of the duke's first words:

> Hath not *old custom* made this life more sweet
> Than that of painted pomp?

a question which would have been absurd had the banishment been recent. From all this we conclude that in Shakespeare's first draft the 'old duke' had been deposed some years before the time of the opening of the play, and that Shakespeare forgot this when writing his expository first scene for his second draft. Furthermore, as we have found good reason for supposing that the prose-section at the beginning of 1. 2. belonged to the revision, there is nothing surprising in a theory that the scene which goes before, and which is also in prose, was written at the same time.

On the other hand, it would be most unsafe to assume with a play so full of ripe poetry as *As You Like It* that the revision was entirely a prose one and that none of the verse belonged to the same rehandling[1]. And as a matter of fact a third inconsistency, of a particularly flagrant character seeing that it concerns the casting of the play for the stage, indicates pretty clearly that the revision was in part a verse one. We have noticed above a verse-passage in 1. 3. which almost certainly belongs to the original draft, since it puts a period of years between the banishment and the beginning of the play. Now 1. 3. falls into three sections dramatically: (i) ll. 1–40, a prose-dialogue between Celia and Rosalind; (ii) ll. 41–89, the episode in which Duke Frederick exiles Rosalind, which is the verse-section containing the passage just spoken of; and lastly (iii) a verse-dialogue between Rosalind and Celia in which they plan their journey. On the analogy of 1. 2., we should expect the first section to have been written at the time of the revision, and assign the second section to the original draft. But what of the third section? The answer depends upon Rosalind's height. At l. 115 she tells us that she is 'more than common tall,' a description which tallies well enough with Oliver's reference to Aliena as 'low' in comparison with her brother Ganymede (4. 3. 87). But at 1. 2. 260, which brings us back again to our unrevised section of 1. 2., we are informed through the mouth of Le Beau that Celia is 'taller' than

---

[1] As little, of course, do we think that the first draft contained no prose; the original version of the play must have been *mainly* verse and the revision very much increased the proportion of prose-lines—that is all we contend.

Rosalind. Clearly Shakespeare changed his mind about
the relative heights of the two girls between the first and
the second draft, and if the passage in 1. 3. represents,
as we think and as every editor has assumed, his final
intention, then the third section of 1. 3. must have been
touched up at the time of the revision.

As it happens, there is another feature of this section
which appears to indicate revision. Lines 106–107 run
as follows:

> *Ros.* Why, whither shall we go?
> *Cel.* To seek my uncle in the forest of Arden.

The high-handed Steevens omitted 'in the forest of
Arden' from this passage, declaring: 'These words are
an evident interpolation, without use, and injurious to
the measure—"Why, whither shall we go?—To seek
my uncle" being a complete verse.' Steevens is right
about the 'injury to the measure' but wrong in regard
to the purpose of the words. It is a remarkable fact that
the word 'Arden' occurs only three times in the whole
play: in the expository first scene (1. 1. 109), here, and
in the prose opening to 2. 4., when it is necessary to
announce to the audience that the weary girls with the
clownish fool have arrived at the forest. Considering
how much the name Arden means in this play, three
references to it can hardly be regarded as a superfluity.
Moreover the third of them occurs after we have been
introduced to the banished duke and his sylvan court in
2. 1. We could therefore very ill dispense with the
second reference, which spoken, as it is, by Celia thirty
lines before 2. 1. opens, acts as a kind of sign-post preparing the audience for what they are to see in the next
scene. If then the words 'in the forest of Arden' be an
interpolation, they were an interpolation by Shakespeare himself who in revising the scene saw that a
sign-post was necessary. But there was another alteration to be made on the same page, for eight lines further

on occurs the passage about Rosalind's stature, which he wrote, we cannot doubt, at the same time as he made the interpolation, perhaps on a slip of paper covering a deleted speech. And if it be asked why this second change was necessary, the answer must be that whereas the Rosalind of the first draft had been played by a short boy, shorter than the boy who took the part of Celia, the Rosalind of the revised and final *As You Like It* was impersonated by a much taller boy—or even perhaps by the same boy a few years later, grown 'nearer heaven...by the altitude of a chopine.'

II. *Date-clues*

The foregoing argument will, we hope, be taken as establishing two probabilities: (i) that the text of *As You Like It* had undergone a drastic revision, which affected the play throughout, before it arrived at the state in which it has come down to us; and (ii) that between these two drafts a sufficient period had elapsed for Shakespeare to have forgotten a good deal about the play, and for the principal boy of his company to have grown taller or to have been superseded. With regard to the dates of these two drafts we have nothing but surmise to offer. It is of course natural to suppose that the second draft belongs to 1599 or thereabouts; but it would not be wise to assume that the text remained entirely unaltered between that date and its publication in 1623. On the other hand, there are several pieces of internal evidence which suggest a date round about 1593 for Shakespeare's first handling of the play. Too much should not be built upon these; but they are worth setting out, pending the discovery of other evidence on the question.

At 3. 5. 81–2 occurs Shakespeare's famous reference to Marlowe:

> Dead Shepherd, now I find thy saw of might,
> 'Who ever loved that loved not at first sight?'—

words which, as Capell first discovered, are a direct reference to *Hero and Leander*, sest. 1, 175–6:

> Where both deliberate, the love is slight:
> Who ever loved that loved not at first sight?

Marlowe became a 'dead shepherd' on 30 May 1593; but *Hero and Leander* was not printed until 1598, so that a quotation from it in a play which was the talk of London in 1599 would be natural enough. On the other hand, the poem was probably already circulating in MS before Marlowe's death and would thus be likely to be known to the 'judicious' among Shakespeare's audience at any time from 1593 onwards. And as it happens recent research renders it quite as probable that the 'Dead Shepherd' passage was written in 1593 as in 1599, since it is now seen to be connected with a second Marlowe reference which it is hard to believe was penned long after the dramatist's death. 'When a man's verses cannot be understood,' remarks Touchstone to Audrey (3. 3. 10), 'nor a man's good wit seconded with the forward child, understanding, it strikes a man more dead than a great reckoning in a little room.' Until 1925 the world was able to take this passage at its face value and might content itself with the paraphrase of Moberly: 'To have one's poetry not understood is worse than the bill of a first-class hotel in a pot-house.' But the discovery by Dr J. L. Hotson[1] of legal documents describing the actual manner of Marlowe's death in what was ostensibly a quarrel in a tavern allows us to put quite another construction upon Touchstone's words. As Mr O. W. F. Lodge, to whom we are indebted for the point, writes in the *Times Literary Supplement* (14 May 1925): 'The documents just discovered show that Marlowe was struck dead on 30 May 1593, in the room of a house at Deptford

[1] *The Death of Christopher Marlowe*, by J. Leslie Hotson, 1925.

Strand by Ingram Frysar in a quarrel over "le reck-nynge,"' and after quoting the lines from *As You Like It* he continues, 'It was the great reckoning in the room of Eleanor Bull's house at Deptford which struck dead the author of the line which Touchstone glances at: "In-finite riches in a little room" (*The Jew of Malta*, I. I. 37).' The suggestion carries conviction, and as Mr Lodge remarks in a subsequent letter (*T.L.S.* 4 June 1925) Touchstone's pointed allusion to the details of the events of 30 May 1593 would have been obvious enough to an audience in 1593 or 1594, but would probably pass quite unnoticed in 1599.

Nor is this the only clue pointing back to the 1592–4 period. Lodge's *Rosalynde*, the novel upon which the play is based, was published in 1590, while Greene's *Orlando Furioso*, which also owes something to Lodge, and with which *As You Like It* has some mysterious but indubitable connexion (cf. note 3. 2. 1–10), was being played in 1592. Furthermore, the figure of Sir Oliver Martext, a Puritan preacher as his name implies, the validity of whose orders Jaques evidently holds in great suspicion, is far more likely to have been put on to the stage in the early nineties when the name of Martin Marprelate was in everyone's mouth and his pamphlets in everyone's hands than at the end of the century when the nickname 'Martext' would awake no such immediate echoes in the public memory. But perhaps the most interesting clue of all is one that links *As You Like It* with the controversy which grew out of the Martin Marprelate affair, viz. the pamphlet war between Nashe and Gabriel Harvey.

Nashe's first direct attack upon Harvey was made in his *Strange Newes* (1593) and the controversy continued until 1599 when it was put a stop to by the authorities, who issued an order, recorded in the Stationers' Register on 1 June of that year, 'that all Nasshes bookes and Doctor Harvyes bookes be taken wheresoeuer they maye be found and that none of theire bookes bee euer printed hereafter.' Fleay[1] thought he detected a reference to this order in Celia's words: 'since the little wit that fools have was silenced, the little foolery that wise men have makes a great show' (1. 2. 83–5). The tedious flyting between the two pamphleteers would be aptly described as 'the little wit that fools have,' and as the passage occurs in the section of 1. 2. which we have dated 1599 on other grounds, Fleay may very well be right in his conjecture, though Celia's expression is vague enough to refer to almost any kind of inhibition, theatrical or literary. We are, however, on more certain ground with ll. 96–113 in 3. 2. wherein Touchstone first describes the rhymes which Rosalind finds upon a tree as 'the right butter-women's rank to market' and then as 'the very false gallop of verses,' and finally asks 'why do you infect yourself with them?' Malone long ago pointed out that 'the very false gallop of verses' could be paralleled in the following passage from Nashe's *Strange Newes*, wherein Harvey's poetic flights are held up to ridicule: 'I would trot a false gallop through the rest of his ragged Verses, but that if I should retort his rime dogrell aright, I must make my verses (as he doth his) run hobling like a Brewers Cart vpon the stones, and obserue no length in their feete; which were *absurdum per absurdius*, to infect my vaine with his imitation[2].' Here we have not merely the coincidence of 'false gallop of verses,' but also (as Furness noticed, though Malone did not) the peculiar use of the word 'infect' in both passages, while the most interesting link of all, which no one has hitherto observed, is that between 'hobling like a Brewers Cart vpon the stones' and 'the right butter-women's rank to market'—a parallel which shows that the borrowing so far from being deliberate on Shakespeare's part was probably

[1] *Life of Shakespeare*, p. 208.
[2] McKerrow, *Nashe*, i. 275.

unconscious. Furness, indeed, perhaps not wholly
seriously, suggests that Shakespeare is referring to the
Harvey-Nashe controversy and indicating 'in terms too
plain to be misunderstood that he sympathised with
Nashe.' We find it impossible to believe that any
audience could have detected the reference had one
been intended, and the unconscious transmutation of a
brewer's cart rumbling upon the stones into a row of
butter-women ambling to market seems to put intention
quite out of the question. There can be no doubt, however, that Shakespeare had been reading *Strange Newes*
shortly before writing this scene in *As You Like It*;
and 2. 2. 8 (v. note) looks like still another echo. Yet
Nashe's pamphlet was seven years old in 1599, and it
is not easy to see how Shakespeare came to be reading
such obsolete journalism in that year, unless he had been
collecting the pamphlets, and the order suppressing them
had renewed his interest in the controversy. Surely it
is far more probable that Touchstone's poetic criticism
was penned in 1593 not many months after the appearance of *Strange Newes,* when Shakespeare like other
people in London would be enjoying the initial
skirmishes in a flyting which had become tedious by
1599. That he was reading the pamphlets at this period
is certain inasmuch as he borrows a jest from Harvey's
Pierce's Supererogation (1593) for *Love's Labour's Lost*
(cf. note 4. 2. 91) and seemingly also from Nashe's
Strange Newes for *The Comedy of Errors* (cf. note
4. 4. 84–5)[1].

Nashe's pamphlet was entered in the Stationers'
Register on 12 January 1593; Marlowe was 'struck
dead' on 30 May following; and, if there be anything
in the foregoing surmises, Shakespeare's first draft of
As You Like It must belong to the summer months of
1593. On this hypothesis it would follow that the

[1] In the note referred to it was assumed that Nashe
borrowed from Shakespeare; we now think differently.

popular play of 1600 was the product of a revision of the 1593 version. Did this revision give us the text exactly as it has come down to us? Substantially, we think, but not entirely. For, we confess to grave suspicions of the Hymen masque in 5. 4., which may well have been added by some writer for the King's Men at any date between 1600 and 1623. It is perhaps worth while recording our impression that the writer in question may have been the unknown dramatist responsible for the non-Shakespearian portions of *Measure for Measure*.

As regards the manuscript which was used as copy by the F. compositors we have nothing very definite to say. That it was prompt-copy of a kind is shown by directions like 'Wraftle' and 'Shout' in 1. 2. but we are very doubtful whether it possessed any very close connexion with Shakespeare's original. Neither the spelling nor the punctuation is strikingly Shakespearian, while one or two curious errors such as 'muft' (much) 2. 1. 49; 'they would' (thy wound) 2. 4. 43; 'defying' (deifying) 3. 2. 355 remind us of the auditory misprints of *Errors* (v. pp. 66–8). Furthermore, the general baldness of the stage-directions and the fact that the text, though demonstrably revised, contains few if any bibliographical clues of textual disturbance point in the direction of transcription, possibly from players' parts.

D. W.

POSTSCRIPT: 1947

I should now reconsider some of the argument from 'verse-fossils' in the light of Sir Edmund Chambers' criticism (*William Shakespeare*, 1930, 1, 233–34), though my experience with *I Henry IV* convinces me that the theory is not so far-fetched as my critic imagines (see *The Origins and Development of Shakespeare's 'Henry IV'* in 'The Library', 4th Ser. XXVI, pp. 14–15). On the other hand, an important article by Mr John Wilcox, entitled 'Putting Jaques into *As You Like It*' in *The Modern Language Review* for 1941 (XXXVI, pp. 388–94) has greatly strengthened the case for a Shakespearian revision.

NOTES

All significant departures from the Folio text, including emendations in punctuation, are recorded; the name of the critic who first suggested a reading being placed in brackets. Illustrative spellings and misprints are quoted from the Good Quarto texts, or from the Folio where no Good Quarto exists. The line-numeration for reference to plays not yet issued in this edition is that used in Bartlett's *Concordance*.

F., unless otherwise specified, stands for the First Folio; T.I. for the Textual Introduction to be found in the *Tempest* volume; Sh. Hand for *Shakespeare's Hand in the play of 'Sir Thomas More'* (Camb. Univ. Press, 1923); Ham. Sp. and Misp. for *Spellings and Misprints in the Second Quarto of Hamlet* (Essays and Studies by members of the English Association, vol. x); N.E.D. for *The Oxford English Dictionary*; Sh. Eng. for *Shakespeare's England*; S.D. for stage-direction; G. for Glossary.

The Title. It has been commonly assumed that the title of this play was suggested to Shakespeare by the sentence 'If you like it, so,' which occurs in the Epistle To The Gentlemen Readers of Lodge's *Rosalynde*. Yet the expression is an exceedingly common one (cf. *Two Gent.* 2. 1. 125), so common that it is not likely to have even caught Shakespeare's eye if he troubled to read Lodge's 'epistle,' which is doubtful. With titles like *Much Ado about Nothing* and *Twelfth Night, or What You Will* belonging to the same period, we need not look for an explanation beyond the dramatist's own mood of gentle banter towards his audience. He plays with the same mood in his Epilogue to the play (v. note Ep. ll. 12–13).

Characters in the Play. F. gives no list of names, which was first supplied by Rowe. The names *Rosalind,*

Adam, *Phebe*, *Ganymede* and *Aliena* are all taken from Lodge, while *Orlando* seems somehow to be associated with the hero of Greene's *Orlando Furioso*, a play based upon Sir John Harington's translation (1591) of Ariosto's poem (cf. note 3. 2. 1–10). The name *Jaques* is also connected with Harington, who in another book, a Rabelaisian advocacy of sanitary reform entitled *The Metamorphosis of Ajax* (1596), not only began the almost universal fashion of the age for quibbles upon Ajax and 'a jakes' (cf. *L.L.L.* 5. 2. 575), but related an entertaining if unseemly story of a mistake made by a bashful waiting-maid in announcing to her mistress the arrival of a certain Mr Jaques Wingfield, which story must have been well known to Shakespeare's audience in 1599. Moreover, seeing that 'melancholy' at this time often stood for 'disagreeable' or even 'unsavoury,' Jaques, as Mr G. B. Harrison[1] has remarked, was 'not an inappropriate name for the melancholy philosopher to whom the Duke said:

> For thou thyself hast been a libertine,
> As sensual as the brutish sting itself,
> And all th'embosséd sores and headed evils,
> That thou with licence of free foot hast caught,
> Wouldst thou disgorge into the general world.'

With Mr Harrison's further suggestion that Shakespeare may have been satirising John Marston in the person of Jaques we find it difficult to agree, if only because Jaques was an 'old gentleman' (cf. 5. 1. 4) and Marston in 1599 a young man of under 25. One of Jaques' speeches, however, seems to owe something to Marston's *Scourge of Villanie*, 1599 (cf. note 2. 7. 70). For *Frederick* v. pp. 98–9; and for *Sir Oliver Martext* v. p. 105 and G. 'Sir'; for *Jaques de Boys* v. note 1. 1. 5. There appears to have been a family named de Boys which held the manor of Weston-in-Arden for several

[1] Marston, *Scourge of Villanie* (Bodley Head Quartos), p. 124.

generations during the middle ages (French, *Shake-speareana Genealogica*, 1869, p. 316).

Acts and Scenes. F. divides into acts and scenes throughout, and the divisions have been followed by all mod. edd.

Punctuation. The F. pointing, though displaying little delicacy, is on the whole fairly good, its principal defect being the frequent use of the period for grammatical rather than dramatic purposes. We record instances of this kind in the notes.

Stage-directions. All original S.D.s are quoted in the notes. They contain nothing that suggests the author's hand, and the one or two hints of costume may be explained as the work of the prompter or book-holder.

I. I.

S.D. F. 'Enter Orlando and Adam.'

2. *fashion: a' bequeathed...but poor thousand* (Dyce and Greg) F. 'faſhion bequeathed...but poore a thouſand'. The absence of a subject in this sentence has excited universal comment, and Dyce plausibly suggested that the missing word was 'a' (= he). If so, the 'a' was probably jerked out of the printer's chase (cf. *L.L.L.* pp. 100–102), together with some kind of stop which is obviously required after 'fashion', and a possible cause for the looseness of type may be found in the necessity for inserting the little ornamental capital A with which F. begins the play. But sometimes printers detect errant type of this kind and when they do they often insert it in the wrong place (cf. *L.L.L.* ut sup.). Dr W. W. Greg suggests (privately) that the 'a' of the clumsy F. 'poore a thouſand' is the missing 'a' of Dyce's conjecture.

5–23. *My brother Jaques...to avoid it* In all this Shakespeare is closely following Lodge, as will be clear from the following extract from *Rosalynde* (ed. Greg, pp. 10–11): '"Let him know little, [meditates Saladyne,

Oliver's prototype, to himself] so shall he not be able to execute much: suppress his wits with a base estate, and though he be a gentleman by nature, yet form him anew, and make him a peasant by nurture: so shalt thou keep him as a slave, and reign thyself sole lord over all thy father's possessions. As for Fernandyne, thy middle brother, he is a scholar and hath no mind but on Aristotle: let him read on Galen while thou riflest with gold, and pore on his book till thou dost purchase lands: wit is great wealth; if he have learning it is enough: and so let all rest." In this humour was Saladyne, making his brother Rosader his foot-boy, for the space of two or three years, keeping him in such servile subjection, as if he had been the son of any country vassal. The young gentleman bore all with patience, till on a day, walking in the garden by himself, he began to consider how he was the son of John of Bordeaux, a knight renowned for many victories, and a gentleman famosed for his virtues; how, contrary to the testament of his father, he was not only kept from his land and entreated as a servant, but smothered in such secret slavery, as he might not attain to any honourable actions.'

5. *Jaques* This is the only occasion on which we learn the name of Sir Rowland's second son. When he appears in person at 5. 4. 147 the F. discreetly, if a little obscurely, describes him as 'Second Brother'; for by this time the audience has come to associate the name Jaques with quite another character. That Shakespeare should use the name twice in this way raises curious speculation. Had he forgotten all about the melancholy Jaques when he began to revise the play? It does not seem likely. Possibly, then, there existed no melancholy Jaques in the first draft, and the conception of him had not yet begun to take form in Shakespeare's brain when the revision of the opening scene was in hand.

at school i.e. at the university; cf. *Ham.* 1. 2. 113.

6. *profit* v. G.

23. S.D. F. 'Enter Oliuer.'

26. *shake me up* v. G. Cf. *Rosalynde* (p. 11), 'Sala-dyne...seeing his brother in a brown study...thought to shake him out of his dumps.'

33–4. *be naught awhile* v. G. 'naught.'

48. *reverence* Why Oliver should take umbrage at this word is not obvious, and Warburton, with Capell's cordial approval, accordingly suggested the emendation 'revenue'. It is certainly attractive, and graphically there is not a minim-stroke's difference between 'reuerence' and 'reuenewe' (the common 16th cent. spelling).

50–1. *you are too young in this* A blow from Oliver (suggested by Staunton) alone makes Orlando's words clear and explains his sudden change of tone.

54. *Sir Rowland de Boys* Cf. *Characters in the Play*, p. 110.

63. *charged you* F. 'charg'd yon'

67. *exercises* v. G.

73. '*will*' We follow a suggestion by Furness and print the word in quotation marks so as to bring out the quibbling reference to the father's will.

80. S.D. F. 'Ex. Orl. Ad.'

81–2. *grow upon me...rankness* v. G. 'grow upon.' There is an implied quibble here: Orlando is growing up, says Oliver; he is an over-grown boy (cf. rankness).

83. S.D. F. 'Enter Dennis.'

89. S.D. F. gives no exit for Dennis.

90. S.D. F. 'Enter Charles.'

92. *Good Monsieur Charles* Walker plausibly suggests that 'morrow' has been omitted after 'good' here. On the other hand the text makes possible sense as it stands.

104. *she would* (F3) F. 'hee would'

109. *the forest of Arden* This is, of course, the scene of the *Rosalynde* story, where it is definitely fixed in France and signifies the Ardennes. But Shakespeare

and still more his audience would throughout the play have the forest of Arden in Warwickshire in mind, and as Furness points out Drayton's description of this forest in his *Polyolbion*, xiii. 13–234, is obviously closely related to Shakespeare's *As You Like It*, though which influenced the other would be difficult to say. According to Meres, Drayton was already 'penning' *Polyolbion* in 1598; the first eighteen books however did not appear before 1612. It is remarkable that the name Arden only occurs three times in the play; cf. p. 102.

132. *by underhand means* v. G. 'underhand.'

146. *anatomize* F. 'anathomize' Cf. *L.L.L.* p. 103, and v. G.

150. *go alone* Charles means 'walk without a crutch.'

151. S.D. F. 'Exit.'

152. *Farewell, good Charles* F. omits the speech-heading before these words.

153. *gamester* v. G.

157. *enchantingly* v. G.

162. S.D. F. 'Exit.'

1. 2.

S.D. F. 'Enter Rofalind, and Cellia.' The spelling 'Cellia' occurs again at l. 2 below but not elsewhere in the text.

2. *Celia*, F. 'Cellia;'

3. *yet I were* (Rowe) F. 'yet were'

11. *righteously tempered* i.e. without alloy; cf. G. 'temper.'

29–31. *Let us sit and mock...equally.* Celia is of course referring to the turn of Rosalind's fortunes.

35–7. *'Tis true...ill-favouredly* Cf. *Ham.* 3. 1. 103–16.

38–9. *thou goest from Fortune's office to Nature's* etc. For this characteristic medieval idea, derived ultimately from Seneca through Boethius, and constantly recurring in Shakespeare, v. Kellett, *Suggestions*, pp. 20–7. The idea is 'that beauty and wit are natural, while money and all our relations to our fellow-men are matters of luck or chance.'

40. S.D. F. 'Enter Clowne.'

41. *No?* (Hanmer) F. 'No;'

50. *and hath* (Malone) F. 'hath'

51. *whetstone* It is rather remarkable that Celia appears to be making no reference to Touchstone's name here. Indeed, the audience do not hear the name until 2. 4. 19, when Rosalind lets it fall quite casually. Is it possible that it was originally only an assumed name like Ganymede and Aliena? The point may have been obscured in the process of revision. Cf. 2. 4. S.D. head-note.

52. *wit! whither wander you?* alluding, of course, to the wandering wits of a 'natural,' and to the Elizabethan phrase 'wit, whither wilt?', commonly addressed to persons who let their tongues run away with them. Cf. 4. 1. 161.

54. *father* F. 'father'

55. *messenger* A common term for pursuivant, a kind of police-officer. Celia retorts to Touchstone's rude manner of address. 'Were you sent to arrest me?' she says in effect. Her words throw some light upon her feeling towards her father.

60–1. *pancakes...mustard* v. G. 'pancake.' The jest, which seems to hint at some host's lame excuse for an ill-cooked dish, is possibly topical.

69–70. The F. brackets admirably bring out the laughing asides.

76. *old Frederick* Cf. pp. 98–9.

78–9. *him. Enough!* F. 'him enough;' Hanmer read 'him: enough!'

83–4. *since the little wit...silenced* Cf. p. 106.

86. *Le Beau* (Steevens) F. 'the Beu'

S.D. F. 'Enter le Beau.' Elsewhere in the scene the F. spelling is always 'Beu'

88. *put on us, as pigeons feed their young* Cf. *L.L.L.* 5. 2. 315 'This fellow pecks up wit, as pigeons pease' (see also G. 'put on'). Le Beau had many resemblances with Boyet. Celia refers of course to Le Beau's mincing speech, who talks with lips pursed, as if they held grains of corn.

90. *news-crammed* Cf. *Ham.* 3. 2. 99 'promise-crammed, you cannot feed capons so.'

91. *the more marketable* Filling the crops of birds just before killing in order to increase their weight is an old poulterer's trick.

marketable. So F.

92. *Bon jour* F. 'Boon-iour' For the F. spelling cf. *L.L.L.* 5. 1. 27–9 (note).

94. *Sport?* Collier 'Spot?' The fact that Collier pretended to find this reading in his 'corrected' Folio does not detract from its value. From l. 88 it is clear that Le Beau articulates mincingly: from ll. 95–102 it is clear that Le Beau is being bamboozled: Collier's emendation, therefore, seems to be the only way of making sense of the passage. It is noteworthy that the weakening or disappearance of the trilled *r* before another consonant was a characteristic of London pronunciation, especially among educated people, in the middle of the 16th cent. (cf. Wyld, *Hist. of Mod. Coll. English*, pp. 298–99). It is possible that Celia's jest was a double one, since 'spot' is a kind of pigeon, though N.E.D. quotes no example of this sense earlier than 1672.

98. *decree* (Pope) F. 'decrees'

99. *laid on with a trowel* The three are still ridiculing Le Beau, and Touchstone is commended for a palpable hit. We can only suppose that in the pompous 'as the Destinies decree' he is aping Le Beau or perhaps some real courtier of whom Le Beau was a caricature

recognisable to Shakespeare's audience. One wonders whether the Knight of the Pancake and Le Beau were one and the same person.

100. *Nay, if I keep not my rank* Touchstone, still aping Le Beau, speaks no doubt haughtily. Rosalind's quibble anticipates a similar one made at Cloten's expense (*Cymb.* 2. 1. 17).

102. *amaze* v. G.

109. *buried?* We add the question-mark, since Celia is clearly asking Le Beau for his tale.

111. *I could match...old tale* Le Beau, she implies, has begun like a nurse telling a fairy-tale.

112–13. *of excellent growth and presence* This is very like Armado's twice-repeated 'men of good repute and carriage' (*L.L.L.* 1. 1. 261–62; 1. 2. 69), and Rosalind ridicules the pompous style by comparing it with that of proclamations, i.e. 'bills' (v. G.). She puns, of course, upon 'presence.' Many commentators see a quibble also in 'bills,' but as Dr Johnson remarks, it is difficult to 'see why Rosalind should suppose that competitors in a wrestling match carried bills on their shoulders.'

127. *day. It* So F.

131–32. *broken music* Generally explained as 'part music,' i.e. music performed by instruments of different classes, which is the technical Elizabethan meaning of the expression (cf. Sh. Eng. ii. 31, 33–4, *Hen. V*, 5. 2. 261–63, *Troil.* 3. 1. 19–21, 53–7). But this interpretation possesses no point at all in the present context; we are persuaded, therefore, that Rosalind means simply a broken musical instrument and refers to the ribs (v. N.E.D. 'rib' 12*a*), i.e. the curved strips of wood which were glued together to form the body of the lute.

138. S.D. F. 'Flourifh. Enter Duke, Lords, Orlando, Charles, and Attendants.'

144–46. *How now*, etc. Cf. pp. 97–8 for the verse-fossils here and throughout this section of the scene.

148. *there is such odds in the man* The emphasis is on 'man'; the Duke thinks of Orlando as 'the youth' (v. l. 139). See G. 'odds.'

156. *I attend them* There is a pretty point here, missed by all the commentators (except, we think, Verity), who dispute as to whether we should read 'her' for 'them' or 'princesses' for 'princess'. To Le Beau, adherent of the usurping Duke, there is only one princess; to Orlando, who belonging to the old party is yet both politic and polite, there are two. It appears from ll. 257–58 below that Orlando does not know them by sight and would therefore not know here that both were present; but ll. 257–58 belong to the unrevised and ll. 156–7 to the revised section of the scene; cf. pp. 97–8.

165–66. *If you saw yourself...your judgement* This has puzzled many and some edd. including Hanmer, Warburton, Capell and Dyce, read 'our' for 'your'. But Celia's meaning is clear: 'You have just seen Charles at work,' she says, 'if you could see *yourself* or would compare your own powers with his' etc.

174. *wherein* i.e. though. Cf. *Wint.* 1. 1. 9; *M.N.D.* 3. 2. 179.

175. *thing. But* So F.

185. *eke* F. 'eeke' Cf. *Temp.* 1. 2. 155 (note).

192. *modest working* Cf. G. 'working.' Orlando uses 'modest' quibblingly: Charles had scoffingly attributed desires to him which were scarcely 'modest' (= decent).

197. *An you mean* (Theobald) F. 'You meane' Clark and Wright plausibly suggest that 'and' (for 'an') 'may have been omitted by the printer, who mistook it for part of the stage-direction—"Orl. and" for "Orland".' We have found many other examples of this kind of misprint; cf. *L.L.L.* p. 110 and notes 2. 1. 211; 4. 1. 143 of the same text.

after, F. 'after:'—clearly the pointing of a compositor misled by F. reading.

201. S.D. F. 'Wraſtle.'

204. S.D. F. 'Shout.'

206–207. *well breathed* v. G. 'breathed.'

218. S.D. F. 'Exit Duke.'

220. *more proud* The comparative renders the sense incomplete; perhaps the sentence was once longer. But the verse just here is poor stuff.

221. *calling* i.e. appellation. There is no parallel recorded for this sense, and we can only suppose that it is a forced usage for metrical reasons.

231. *love* F. 'loue;' The F. pause may be deliberate, since the word 'love' uttered at this particular moment is heavy with dramatic significance. Celia speaks what Rosalind hides in her heart.

232. *exceeded promise* (Capell) F. 'exceeded all promiſe'

236. *Shall we go, coz?* None of the sentimentalists has observed the force of this sudden question, which is quite as expressive as Orlando's inability to stammer out thanks: the two have exchanged glances, and what Rosalind has seen 'nets her in her blushes, and wounds her, and tames'—no wonder she wants to run away, at first.

237–39. *My better parts...lifeless block* v. G. 'quintain.' Orlando had been a brave figure before meeting Rosalind in Love's lists. That encounter has stripped him of his outward panoply and left him nothing but a dumb post.

239. *lifeless* F. 'liueleſſe'—the usual Shakespearian spelling.

244. S.D. F. 'Exit.'

246. S.D. F. 'Enter Le Beu.' In this Le Beau who talks verse there is not a trace of the affected fop who talked prose earlier in the scene; the character seems to have developed into the fop in the course of revision; cf. pp. 98–101.

251. *love,* F. 'loue;'

253. *misconsters* the old form of 'misconstrues'

260. *the smaller* (Malone) F. 'the taller' Cf. pp. 101–103. Rowe read 'shorter', which sounds ugly before 'daughter'

274. S.D. F. gives no exit.

277. *Rosalind* F. 'Rosaline'
S.D. F. 'Exit.'

I. 3.

S.D. F. 'Enter Celia and Rosaline.' Our authority for the 'couch' is 'laid up' (l. 7). The atmosphere and dialogue of the first 40 lines of this scene are extraordinarily like those of the scene in Hero's bedroom (*Ado*, 3. 4.).

9. *mad* Furness shrewdly asks, 'Is this word quite above suspicion?' Some expression is needed to balance 'lamed', and the word, we think, may be *mauled*, which in the common 16th cent. spelling 'mald' might easily be misread as 'madd'. Cf. Sh. Hand. p. 94 and Ham. Sp. and Misp. p. 45. The word 'rule' is not unlike 'ride' in l. 100 of the 'Shakespearian' Addition to *Sir Thomas More*.

14. *holiday foolery* in retort to 'working-day world.' *the trodden paths* from which the princesses had strayed in holding conversation with an unknown wrestler.

18. *Hem them away* i.e. cough them away. Celia is quibbling upon 'bur'; v. G.

19. *cry 'hem' and have him* Rosalind quibbles both on 'him' and 'cry': 'I would try, if I could have him by "crying" him round the town like something lost, stolen or strayed,' she says in effect. Possibly she is glancing also at the 'crying' of banns in church.

24–5. *O, a good wish...despite of a fall* The jest that lies beneath this wrestler's patter is unexplained, but clearly it is 'woman's talk' of some kind, probably in reference to child-birth.

31. *chase* i.e. sequence. Celia is no doubt, as Furness notes, led to use the word 'chase' because of 'ensue', just before: cf. 'seek peace and ensue it.'

35. *Why should I not? doth he not deserve well?* Capell and Dyce omitted the first 'not' and so made the text intelligible, but, as Furness justly observes, 'at the cost of all archness or irony.' We must be content to leave the passage unexplained, like that just noted at ll. 24–5.

37. S.D. F. 'Enter Duke with Lords.'—after l. 35.

41. *with your safest haste* i.e. with all the haste your safety demands.

57. *likelihood* (F2) F. 'likelihoods'

70. *remorse* v. G.

71. *I was too young* etc. Cf. p. 100.

75. *Juno's swans* Aldis Wright draws attention to the fact that the swan was sacred to Venus and not to Juno; Dr Percy Simpson notes (privately) that Kyd makes the same mistake in *Soliman and Perseda*, 4.1.70.

77. *smoothness,* F. 'fmoothnes;'

78. *her patience* F. 'per patience'

83. *doom* F. 'doombe'

89. S.D. F. 'Exit Duke, &c.'

102. *your change* Some follow F2 and read 'your charge'

104. *pale,* F. 'pale;'

107. *To seek...forest of Arden.* A prose-line in the midst of verse: omit the words 'in the forest of Arden' and the verse is unimpaired. Clearly there has been adaptation at this point. Cf. p. 102.

117–18. *curtle-axe...boar-spear* The forester's weapons, meet for Arden.

120. *martial* F. 'marshall'—a common Shake-spearian spelling.

125. *Ganymede* F. 'Ganimed' Cf. *Rosalynde*, p. 34 'Thus fitted to the purpose, away go these two friends,

having now changed their names, Alinda being called Aliena, and Rosalynde Ganymede.'

126. *be called* F. 'by call'd'

137. *go we in* (F2) F. 'go in we'

138. S.D. F. 'Exeunt.'

2. 1.

S.D. F. 'Enter Duke Senior: Amyens, and two or three Lords like Forreſters.'

1. *exile,* F. 'exile:'

2. *old custom* This implies a lengthy period of exile, and therefore contradicts the implications of the conversation between Oliver and Charles in 1. 1. Cf. p. 100.

5–6. *Here feel we not...The seasons' difference?* F. 'Heere feele we not...the ſeaſons difference,' Theobald read 'but' for 'not' and has been followed by all mod. edd. In 1914, however, Prof. Grierson (*Mod. Lang. Rev.* ix. pp. 370–72) vindicated the F. text by pointing out (i) that the Duke is not making an assertion, as all edd. have assumed, but asking a third rhetorical question, (ii) that the F. compositor has quite naturally omitted the mark of interrogation, because the question passes into a statement. (As a matter of fact the passage is very difficult to punctuate, and we have had to be content with a kind of makeshift), (iii) that the whole point of the Duke's argument, the text upon which he bases his discourse, 'Sweet are the uses of adversity,' is obscured by changing 'not' into 'but'. Instead of complaining, as Theobald would make him, of 'the penalty of Adam,' he reckons the fact that he does feel the penalty as one of the greatest boons of sylvan life. According to tradition 'the seasons' difference' is one of the results of Adam's fall: in Eden it was perpetual spring.

12. *uses* v. G.

13. *venomous* The popular belief in the venom of toads goes back to Pliny.

14. *jewel in his head* The toadstone, 'of power to repulse poysons, and...a most sovereign medicine for the stone' (Ed. Fenton, *Secrete Wonders of Nature*, 1569), was part of the lapidary lore of the age, and of course finds its place in Lyly's *Euphues*: 'the foule Toade hath a faire stone in his head' (Bond, *Works of Lyly*, i. 202).

18. *I would not change it* F. gives these words to Amiens; Dyce first restored them to the Duke, to whom they assuredly belong. Both rhythmically and poetically they crown the speech. Moreover, Amiens's words show him as less content than the Duke.

23. *burghers* Cf. Drayton, *Polyolbion*, xviii. 65–6 'Where, fearless of the hunt, the hart securely stood,/ And everywhere walk'd free, a burgess of the wood'; and *Arcadia*, 1590 (ed. Feuillerat), p. 264 'the wild burgesses of the forest'.

24. *confines* v. G. and cf. l. 63 below.

forkéd heads i.e. arrows. v. G.

33–43. *To the which...Augmenting it with tears* Cf. *Ham*. 3. 2. 282 'Why, let the stricken deer go weep,' and Drayton, *Polyolbion*, xiii. 110–61, which describes a hunt in Arden and concludes with a reference to the tears of the dying stag. See also *Arcadia, ibid*. p. 61: 'the poore beast, who with teares shewed the unkindnesse he took of man's crueltie'.

40. *fool* v. G.

42. *th'extremest verge* the very edge.

45. *similes*. F. 'fimilies.'

46. *in* (Pope) F. 'into' As Malone suggested the F. 'into' has probably been caught by the compositor's eye from the line immediately above.

49. *much* (F2) F. 'muft'

50. *friends* (Rowe) F. 'friend'

59. *the country* (F2) F. 'Countrie'

62. *kill them up* We should say 'kill them off'

67. *cope* v. G.

69. S.D. F. 'Exeunt.'

2. 2.

S.D. F. 'Enter Duke, with Lords.'

8. *the roynish clown* Cf. Nashe, *Strange Newes* (1593), 'clownish and roynish ieasts' (McKerrow, i. p. 324), v. p. 107.

13. *wrestler* A trisyllable—suggestive of early Shakespearian verse; cf. *Two Gent.* 1. 3. 84; 2. 4. 208 (notes).

21. S.D. F. 'Exeunt.'

2. 3.

S.D. F. 'Enter Orlando and Adam.'

1. *Who's there?* This abrupt opening to the scene, with a short line, suggests adaptation.

2–8. These ejaculations of delight mingled with misgivings are very attractive. Adam is a character unique in Shakespeare and reminds us of Joe in *Great Expectations*.

8. *bonny prizer* v. G.

9. *before you.* So F.

10. *some* (F2) F. 'ſeeme'—an *o:e* misprint.

16. *Why, what's the matter?* F. prints this as part of Adam's first speech but prefixes 'Ad.' correctly to 'O unhappy youth.'

17. *within this roof* The expression is normal Elizabethan English, but Capell conjectured 'beneath this roof' because of the awkwardness of two 'withins' in the same line.

29. *Why, whither, Adam* etc. F. prefixes 'Ad.' to this line, though the same prefix stands rightly at the beginning of l. 30.

37. *diverted blood* v. G.

58. *meed* According to Furness, some copies of F. read 'neede' here.

71. *seventeen* (Rowe) F. 'ſeauentie'

76. S.D. F. 'Exeunt.'

2. 4.

S.D. F. 'Enter Roſaline for Ganimed, Celia for Aliena, and Clowne, alias Touchstone.' This 'Clowne alias Touchstone' lends support to the idea that 'Touchstone' was originally intended to be an assumed name like Ganymede. Cf. note 1. 2. 51.

1. *weary* (Theobald) F. 'merry' Graphically 'weary' and 'merry' might easily be confused, since both 'wery' and 'mery' are good Shakespearian spellings (cf. *Son.* 7. 9; *2 Hen. IV*, 4. 2. 81, etc.). And Touchstone's reply to Rosalind seems to make Theobald's reading certain.

12. *bear no cross* a quibble; v. G. 'cross.'

18–20. *Ay,/Be so...here/A young...talk.* F. prints this as prose: Walker first discovered it to be verse, and the discovery suggests that the prose of this scene belongs to a later stage of the play's history than the verse. Cf. pp. 94–8.

20. S.D. F. 'Enter Corin and Siluius.'

28. *so—* F. 'so:'

32. *ne'er* (Rowe) F. 'neuer'

37. *Wearing* an obsolete form of 'wearying'

42. S.D. F. 'Exit.'

43. *searching of* v. G. 'search.'
thy wound (Rowe) F. 'they would'

48. *batler* v. G. F2 and all later texts read 'batlet'

50. *wooing of a peascod* Peascods were regarded as lucky gifts by rustic lovers in old times, and Halliwell quotes Browne, *Britannia's Pastorals*, 11. iii. 93–6 'The peascod greene oft with no little toyle/Hee'd seeke for in the fattest fertil'st soile,/And rend it from the stalke to bring it to her,/And in her bosome for

acceptance wooe her.' But Touchstone's jest about taking 'two cods' (v. G.) from one 'peascod' is probably connected with the word 'codpiece.' Cf. *M.W.W.* 1.1.20 (note). He seems to be quibbling upon 'stone' (l. 46) in the same way.

54. *mortal in folly* i.e. 'abounding in folly' (Johnson); v. G. 'mortal.'

55. *wiser* Rosalind probably takes 'mortal' in the sense of 'deadly.' Singer suggests that perhaps Rosalind 'has in her mind that possession is the grave of love, which expires in its own folly.'

56. *ware* v. G.

63. *clown* It is Touchstone's cue to play the courtier in Arden and to treat all its inhabitants as 'clowns.'

66. *you, friend* (F2) F. 'your friend'

78. *recks* (Hanmer) F. 'wreakes'

79. *hospitality:* F. 'hoſpitalitie.'

80. *bounds of feed* limits of pasturage, cf. 3.5.107.

91–2. F. divides 'And...wages:/ I like...could / Waste...in it.'

96. *feeder* i.e. shepherd, v. G. Corin was attached to the farm and would become shepherd to the next owner; for though villeinage was theoretically extinct in Elizabethan times, labour was practically immobile (v. Tawney, *Agrarian Problem in the* 16*th cent.*, pp. 42–3). The point of Corin's words seems hitherto to have escaped notice. But v. Sh. Eng. i. 365.

97. S.D. F. 'Exeunt.'

2. 5.

S.D. F. 'Enter Amyens, Iaques, & others.'

1. The song is simply headed 'Song' in F. and is not assigned to any character, though it is of course obvious that Amiens sings it.

3. *turn* v. G.

12–14. *I thank it* etc. F. prints this and several

others of Jaques' speeches in this scene as if they were verse.

20–1. *I care not for their names, they owe me nothing* v. G. 'names.' Jaques is quibbling: 'I do not require their signatures to my bond' is the meaning he hints at. The same jest is to be found at *L.L.L.* 2. 1. 197–98 'I desire her name./She hath but one for herself—to desire that were a shame.'

25. *dog-apes;* F. 'dog-Apes.' v. G.

26–7. *a penny...beggarly thanks* i.e. the thanks are profuse out of all proportion to the value of the gift; 'beggarly' = like a beggar. Cf. *Ham.* 2. 2. 280–82.

29–30. *cover the while* i.e. prepare the table.

31. *to look you* i.e. to look for you.

33. *disputable* i.e. disputatious.

36. F. heads the second stanza 'Song. Altogether heere.'

37. *to live i'th' sun* v. G. 'sun.'

41–3. *Here...weather* F. 'Heere ſhall he ſee, etc.'

45. *in despite of my invention* i.e. just to spite my imagination.

47. *Thus it goes* F. heads this 'Amy.', like the speeches that precede and follow it. F2 gave it to Jaques. If Jaques hands Amiens a paper, the latter would sing the song, as he promises, from it, whereas with the F2 text Jaques' version is not sung at all, unless it be comically by Jaques himself, as some have supposed.

52. *ducdame*—a trisyllable, to rhyme with 'come to me.' The word is one of those textual cruxes in Shakespeare to which great attention has been given, Furness' *Variorum* edition devoting three pages to it. The probable if not certain solution has now however been known for some years though it has not as yet, we believe, been set forth completely in print. The word is in short a corruption or mishearing of the Romani *dukrá mẽ*, which became *dukdá me* by the not infrequent change of

r to *d*, these letters being closely connected in pronunciation in Romani. The expression, which means 'I foretell, I tell fortunes or prophesy,' fits the context perfectly. As the call of the Gipsy fortune-teller at fairs or public gatherings, it is a 'Greek (= sharper's) invocation to call fools into a circle' (v. G. 'Greek'). The interpretation also renders the reference to 'the first-born of Egypt' intelligible. We owe the substance of this note to the kindness of Dr John Sampson, the learned librarian of the University of Liverpool, who is responsible for the Romani derivation, and who draws our attention to an article in the 1st Series of the *Journal of the Gypsy Lore Society* (vol. iii. pp. 96–9), in which Mr Charles Strachey first developed the theory that the word was of Gipsy origin.

The point of Jaques' skit upon Amiens' song is now obvious: the members of the banished court are so many amateur Gipsies, forced to lead this uncomfortable life by the 'stubborn will' of the Duke, who as the elder brother is 'the first-born of Egypt.'

60. *seek the duke* The Duke, it will be remembered, went to find Jaques at the end of 2. 1. In 2. 7. he is back again, having failed in his quest.

60–1. *his banquet is prepared* Where was the table prepared in Shakespeare's theatre? Not on the front stage, otherwise the next scene would be ridiculous. We must suppose, therefore, that the inner-stage was not the Duke's cave but 'this tree' (l. 30), and that at the end of the scene the curtain was drawn to conceal the banquet, which was again revealed at the beginning of 2. 7. *banquet* v. G.

61. S.D. F. 'Exeunt.'

2. 6.

S.D. F. 'Enter Orlando, & Adam.'

The whole scene is printed by F. as if it were verse, but the line-arrangement is almost certainly due, as

Furness points out, to the printer, who beginning p. 193
of the F. with Scene 7 is obliged to spread out Scene 6
in order to carry on to the foot of p. 192 and so avoid
the awkwardness of having the heading 'Scena Septima'
at the bottom of a page. On the other hand, quite apart
from all this, it is clear that the scene was originally in
verse which has been revised as prose (cf. pp. 94–8). It
opens, for example, with the following lines of fossil-
verse:

> *Adam.* Dear master,
> I can [go] no further: O, I die for food.
> Here lie I down, and measure out my grave.
> Farewell, kind master.
> *Orlando.*   Why, how now, Adam!
> No greater heart in thee? Live *yet* a little,
> Comfort a little, cheer thyself a little.
> If this *wild* forest *any thing savage yield*.

9. *comfortable* v. G.
19. S.D. F. 'Exeunt.'

2. 7.

S.D. F. 'Enter Duke Sen. & Lord, like Out-lawes.'
Cf. 'like Forresters' at head of 2. 1.—both costume-
directions. Most edd. give Amiens an entry at the
beginning of this scene, because he is needed for the
song at the end. But as he went out to find the Duke at
the end of 2. 5., if he re-entered with him now the first
lines of the scene would be ridiculous. We therefore
give him a silent entry with Jaques at l. 7.

For *fruit and wine* v. G. 'banquet' and l. 98 below.

5. *compact of jars* composed of discords.

7. S.D. F. 'Enter Iaques.'

11. short line. Capell supposed that the beginning
of the line had been lost, and notes that l. 10 ends with
a comma in F.

13. *motley* v. G. Jaques distinguishes; the 'motley'
fool was one of two kinds of fool. *a miserable world!*

F. '(a miſerable world:)' We suspect that this parenthesis should read 'ah, miserable world', the spelling
'a' for 'ah' being a common one of the period and
frequent in F. and Qq. Certainly 'ah, miserable
world!' would be a most natural exclamation for
Jaques as he holds his sides, sore with laughing 'sans
intermission an hour.'

34. *O worthy fool!* F. 'A worthy foole:' 36. *A
worthy fool...* F. 'O worthie Foole:' This interchange,
first recorded as an anonymous conjecture by Clark
and Wright, is pronounced *emendatio certissima* by
Furness. The compositor's eye, confused by the similar
opening to the two lines, must be held responsible for
the F. reading, though perhaps his confusion was as-
sisted by Shakespeare's habit of making his *a*'s and *o*'s
alike.

39. *biscuit* The seaman's allowance of victuals
per day in Shakespeare's time was a gallon of beer
and a pound of biscuit (Sh. Eng. i. 167).

40. *voyage, he* F. 'voyage: He' *places* v. G.

44. *my only suit* Jaques quibbles.

52. *'why'...way* He quibbles again.

55. *Not to seem* (Theobald) F. 'Seeme' The sense
seems to require Theobald's additional words, and the
metre shows that some words have been lost. The F.
reading has, of course, found its defenders; but the
emendation is now accepted by most mod. edd. A
good illustration of the loss of the first two or three
words in a line by an accident of the press may be
found in *M. of V.* 4. 1. 71–2 (v. note).

bob: if F. 'bob. If'

57. *squand'ring glances* random hits.

64. *chiding sin:* F. 'chiding ſin.'

66. *sting* v. G.

67. *embossèd...headed* v. G.

70. *Why, who cries out on pride,* A short line.
Jaques makes no reply to the Duke's personal attack, and

what he says reads like an illustration to some general
argument which does not appear. We suspect a 'cut'
here. 'Jaques appears either wilfully or through
shallowness to miss the deep wisdom of the Duke's
saying and the whole character of his admonition. The
Duke had not said that Jaques would "offend" people,
but that he would "corrupt" them' (Moberly).
Mr G. B. Harrison (Bodley Head Quartos, xiii) draws
attention to the close similarity of Jaques' argument in
this speech to that of the prose-epilogue to Marston's
Scourge of Villanie (1599). 'Let this protestation,'
Marston concludes, 'satisfie our curious searchers. So
may I obtayne my best hopes, as I am free from en-
deuouring to blast any private mans good name. If any
one (forced with his owne guilt) will turne it home and
say *Tis I*, I cannot hinder him. Neyther doe I iniure
him.' Cf. *Characters in the Play*, p. 110.

73. *the weary very means* F. 'the wearie verie
meanes' Generally admitted to be corrupt, though no
satisfactory emendation has been suggested. Attention
has been chiefly concentrated upon 'wearie verie'
whereas the corruption in our view lies in 'meanes',
which we take to be a misprint for *mints*. This would
give an excellent reading: the very mints cannot issue
coin fast enough for the extravagance of the age, says
Jaques. We have found an identical misprint at
Meas. 2. 4. 48 (v. note), 'ment' was a 16th cent.
spelling of 'mint', and 'ments' might easily be mistaken for 'menes' (=means), the *t:e* confusion being
frequent in Qq. (cf. Ham. Sp. and Misp. p. 45).
Wright, following Singer, read 'wearer's' for 'wearie'
in his Clarendon edition, quoting *Hen. VIII*, 1. 1. 83–5
and Stubbes' *Anatomie of Abuses* on the spending of
fortunes by Elizabethans upon clothes. The proposal
is ingenious, but hardly fits the context. After 'Doth it
not flow as hugely as the sea?' a reference to the loss
of a 'private party's' means is not only an anticlimax

but something of a contradiction. Jaques' point is that pride is a universal disease, which threatens national, not merely individual, bankruptcy.

80. *says his bravery is not on my cost* i.e. says I haven't got to pay his tailor's bill.

83. *There then!—how then? what then?* i.e. There you are! What do you make of that?

84. *if it do him right* i.e. if the cap fits.

87. *any man. But who comes* (F2) F. 'any. man But who come'

S.D. F. 'Enter Orlando.'

96. *inland bred* v. G. 'inland.'

100–103. F. divides '*Iaq*. And you...with reaſon/I muſt dye. *Du. Sen.* What would you have?/Your gentleneſſe...your force/Moue vs to gentleneſſe.' The irregular lining and Jaques' prose-speech in the middle of a verse-scene point to revision or abridgment.

100. *reason* 'We should possibly read *reasons*. Here, as in other places, Shakespeare evidently indulged in the perennial pun on "reasons" and "raisins"' (Staunton).

109. *commandment.* So F.

117. *pitied*, F. 'pittied:'   118. *be:* F. 'be,'— transposed pointing.

127. *while*, F. 'while:'

133. *out*, F. 'out.'

135. F. gives no 'exit.'

137. *This wide and universal theatre* These words and the famous speech that follows suggest, says Fleay (*Life*, p. 209), 'a date subsequent to the building of the Globe, with its motto "Totus mundus agit histrionem".' The building was completed in the summer of 1599.

139–66. *All the world's a stage* etc. It is well to remember that this brilliant passage—one of the best-known in all literature—is a piece of sheer cynicism, thoroughly in keeping with the speaker's character, but certainly not to be taken as Shakespeare's own sentiment, as it too often is. The idea of the seven ages was a commonplace of the period.

144. *Mewling* i.e. mewing like a cat. v. G. 'mewl.'

147. *school:* F. 'fchoole.'

149. *eyebrow:* F. 'eye-brow.'

154. *with good capon lined* v. G. 'capon.'

156. *modern instances* trite illustrations, v. G.

164. *history* chronicle-play.

166. S.D. F. 'Enter Orlando with Adam.' There is a well-known tradition derived from Oldys the 18th cent. antiquary, that one of Shakespeare's brothers, presumably Gilbert, used in old age to recall how his brother once acted 'a part in one of his own comedies, wherein, being to personate a decrepit old man, he wore a long beard, and appeared so weak and drooping and unable to walk, that he was forced to be supported and carried by another person to a table, at which he was seated among some company, who were eating, and one of them sung a song.' Upon which reported spectacle Coleridge thus moralises: 'Think of the scene between him and Orlando; and think again, that the actor of that part had to carry the author of that play in his arms! Think of having had Shakespeare in one's arms! It is worth having died two hundred years ago to have heard Shakespeare deliver a single line.' Surely this is the very ecstasy of bardolatry.

167–68. F. prints this as prose, which fact and the broken line (168) suggest revision or adaptation. It is perhaps worth noting that 'feed' rhymes with 'need' (l. 169).

174. *Blow, blow,* etc. F. heads this 'Song' and assigns it to no character.

176. *ingratitude:* F. gives no stop here, but edd. are no doubt justified in borrowing the colon from the corresponding line in stanza 2.

178. *Because thou art not seen* i.e. 'thou art an enemy that dost not brave us with thy presence, and whose

unkindness is therefore not aggravated by insult' (Dr Johnson).

180. *Hey-ho* F. 'Heigh-ho' We adopt the variant spelling to avoid confusion with 'heigh-ho,' the sigh. v. G. *holly* 'the emblem of mirth' (Halliwell).

182. *Then hey-ho* (Rowe) F. 'The heigh ho'

196. *effigies* v. G.

201. *master* (F2) F. 'masters'

203. S.D. F. 'Exeunt.'

3. 1.

S.D. F. 'Enter Duke, Lords, & Oliuer.'

6. *Seek him with candle* A reference to *Luke* xv. 8.

10. *seize* v. G.

12. short line.

18. *turn him going* i.e. set him packing.

S.D. F. 'Exeunt.'

3. 2.

S.D. F. 'Enter Orlando.'

1–10. *Hang there*, etc. There is a curious similarity at this point to a scene in the famous *Orlando Furioso* by Robert Greene (staged c. 1592, printed in a garbled version 1594). In both plays the lady's name is carved upon the bark of trees and poems in her honour hung upon their boughs; but in Greene's the work is accomplished by an enemy of Orlando's to inspire him with jealousy. It is noticeable that the incident is prefaced in both by an impassioned invocation by Orlando to some heavenly body: in Greene to Venus ('Thou gladsome lamp that wait'st on Phoebe's train'), in Shakespeare to Phoebe herself. These coincidences, which can hardly be accidental, establish a connexion of some sort or other between the two plays.

2–3. *queen of night...from thy pale sphere above* From this it is clear that Orlando is speaking at night; but there is nothing to support this later on in the scene.

Indeed Rosalind's question 'What is't o'clock?' and Orlando's retort 'You should ask me what time o'day: there's no clock in the forest' (ll. 297–99) make it impossible that they should be speaking at night. It is, therefore, night-time in the verse opening of the scene and day-time in the prose sequel; and the inconsistency once again points to revision. Cf. pp. 98–102.

2. *thrice-crownèd* Cf. 'the triple Hecate' *M.N.D.* 5. 1. 382 (note).

4. *that my full life doth sway* Cf. *Twelfth Night,* 2. 5. 118 'M.O.A.I. doth sway my life.' v. G. 'sway.'

10. *unexpressive* v. G.

S.D. F. 'Exit.'/'Enter Corin & Clowne.'

15. *naught.*
16. *life.* } So F.
18. *tedious.*
20. *stomach.*

24. *friends;* F. 'frends.'

26. *good pasture* F. 'pood pasture'

28. *complain of* i.e. complain of the lack of. Cf. 2. 4. 72 'faints for succour.'

30. *natural philosopher* v. G.

35–6. *like an ill-roasted egg* etc. Those who have not been to Court are only half-baked. Corin may be a 'natural philosopher' but without 'good manners,' which must be learnt at Court, he is one-sided only.

39. *manners* v. G.

46. *court.* So F.

49. *instance* v. G.

57. *sooner.* So F.

65. *cat.* So F.

69–70. *incision...raw* Usually explained as a reference to the old method of cure by blood-letting; but 'raw' means 'in the natural state, uncultivated, untutored' (viz. just the qualities which Master Courtier Touchstone found in these rustic clowns), while 'incision' was at this period often used for 'insition' (=engrafting; v. N.E.D.). We take it therefore that Touchstone means: 'May God graft thee! Thou art but a wild stock.'

71. *eat*, F. 'eate:'

72. *wear*, F. 'weare;'

73. *happiness*, F. 'happineſſe:'

81. *match*. So F.

85. S.D. F. 'Enter Roſalind.'

90. *lined* v. G. 'line.'

92. *face* S. Walker conjectured 'fair' which in the sp. 'fare' is graphically possible.

96–7. *the right butter-women's rank to market* i.e. the rhymes, which are all the same, follow each other like a line of butter-women jogging along to market. Cf. note ll. 112–13 below. Aldis Wright ingeniously conjectured that 'rank' should be 'rack' i.e. 'a horse's gait in which the two feet on each side are lifted almost simultaneously, and the body is left entirely without support between the lifting of one pair and the landing of the other' (N.E.D.). This kind of jogging pace would suit butter-women, but seems to have little point in the present context.

104. *Winter* (F3) F. 'Wintred'.

107. *to cart* v. G. 'cart.'

112–13. *false gallop of verses...infect yourself with them?* Cf. pp. 105–107. Possibly Nashe, from whom Shakespeare borrowed the phrase 'false gallop,' is quibbling upon 'riding rhyme,' the contemporary name for the Chaucerian heroic couplet.

114–15. *Peace, you dull fool* etc. A line of verse.

117. *I'll graff it with you* Rosalind is, of course, quibbling upon 'yew' as she quibbles upon 'med-dler' and 'medlar' in the next line.

118–19. *then it will be the earliest fruit i'th' country* 'If the medlar were graffed with the forward-ness of the clown, instead of being one of the latest it

would be "the earliest fruit i'th' country" and rotten
before it was half ripe' (Collier).

122. S.D. F. 'Enter Celia with a writing.'

123-24. *Peace* etc. F. prints this as prose; Capell
first arranged as verse. A piece of fossil-verse; cf.
ll. 114-15 above and pp. 94-8.

125. *a desert* (Rowe) F. 'Deſert'

128. *show* F. 'ſhoe'—an eye-rhyme with 'Noe'
(l. 126).

132. *age;* F. 'age.'

136. *end,* F. 'end;'

139-44. *The quintessence...distilled* The train of
thought is astrological, v. G. 'quintessence.' Furness,
we think rightly, interprets 'in little' as a reference to
the microcosm, man—the 'little world of man' (*Lear,*
3. 1. 10).

140. *show.* So F.

143. *enlarged:* F. 'enlarg'd,'

145. *her heart* (Rowe) F. 'his heart'

147. *Atalanta's better part* i.e. her fleetness of
foot, but not her greed. Cf. 'Helen's cheek, but not her
heart.' We owe this note to a suggestion by Dr Greg.

155. *pulpiter* (Spedding: Clark and Wright)
F. 'Iupiter' Spedding's emendation, now adopted by
most edd., fits the context perfectly. The epithet 'gentle,'
ludicrous as applied to Jupiter, is obviously directed to
Celia, while 'tedious homily' and 'parishioners' lend
'pulpiter' strong support. We may add that there is no
serious difficulty from the graphical point of view,
since an 'English' *p* (of the 'second class,' v. plate vi,
Sh. Hand, p. 96) might be mistaken for a capital *I* if
the loop were blind.

159. *back-friends!* F. 'backe friends:' All edd.
read 'back, friends!' as if it were a command, but make
no attempt to explain. **Celia** turns at Rosalind's speech,
and sees the trio lurking behind the tree at her back.
For 'back-friend' v. G. and cf. *Errors,* 4. 2. 37.

162. *bag and baggage* No doubt intended as an unmannerly reference to Rosalind and Celia, while we give a meaning to 'scrip and scrippage' if we suppose that Touchstone picks up Celia's paper and puts it into his scrip or wallet.

163. S.D. F. 'Exit.'

176. *palm-tree* Commentators marvel at this 'palm-tree' in Arden, and some interpret as the goat-willow, which is still called 'palm' by most English children; but is it anything more than a jest of Rosalind's? Palm is the symbol of victory, and it was her triumph. Moreover, she had 'found' the verses in full view of the audience and 'palm' (in either sense) would hardly suit one of the stage-pillars.

176–77. *be-rhymed since Pythagoras' time...Irish rat* It was a superstition among the Irish peasantry that their bards could rhyme rats to death, and this became a stock joke with English writers. Ireland was very much in the minds of Londoners when *As You Like It* was taking final shape; cf. note 5. 2. 104–105. For 'Pythagoras' v. G.

184–85. *friends...mountains* alluding to the proverb 'Friends may meet but mountains never greet' (Steevens). Malone compares *Mother Bombie*, 5. 3 'Then wee foure met, which argued wee were no mountains.'

193. *hooping* v. G. 'hoop.'

194. *Good my complexion!* i.e. my poor dear blushes!

197. *a South-sea of discovery* This has puzzled many because they have not observed that 'discovery' has two sides to it, (*a*) disclosure, (*b*) exploration. 'One minute's delay,' protests Rosalind, 'is as tedious to me as a voyage across the South Seas is to explorers seeking Eldorado.' Volumes of 16th cent. travel are compressed into Rosalind's metaphor.

201. *at all.* So F.

204. *Is he of God's making?* or his tailor's (Aldis Wright). Cf. *Lear*, 2. 2. 60.

212–13. *speak sad brow and true maid* Cf. l. 271 'answer you right painted cloth,' and for similar idioms *King John*, 2. 1. 462; *Hen.V*, 5. 2. 156; *Tw.Nt.* 1. 5. 115. For 'sad' v. G.

219. *Wherein went he?* How was he dressed?

223. *Gargantua's mouth* v. G. 'Gargantua.' Some have doubted whether Shakespeare had read Rabelais, but if he was at all intimate with Florio, the translator of Montaigne and a 'servant' of the Earl of Southampton, he must have heard much talk about him. The use of the name Holofernes for the schoolmaster in *L.L.L.* is another sign of acquaintanceship.

225. *To say ay and no* i.e. just to answer 'yes' and 'no' to all your questions.

232. *relish* v. G.

observance. So F. v. G. 'observance.'

234. *Jove's tree* Cf. *Temp.* 5. 1. 45 'Jove's stout oak.'

235. *drops such fruit* (Cap. + C.J.S.) F. 'dropped forth fruite'. *Forth* gives wrong sense.

238. *There lay he* etc. 'Celia is speaking in a mock-romantic, satirical-sentimental style' (Verity).

240. *Though it be pity* etc. Rosalind speaks, as it were 'painted cloth' (cf. l. 271 below), to be in keeping with Celia's style, quibbling of course upon 'ground.'

242. *thy tongue* (Rowe) F. 'the tongue'

244. *heart* F. 'hart' The quibble is obvious.

245. *burthen* v. G.

248. S.D. F. 'Enter Orlando & Jaques.'

251–56. *I thank you* etc. Note these six lines of verse suddenly appearing in the midst of prose; cf. pp. 94–8.

255. *God buy you* v. G. Here as often a dissyllable.

262. *just* v. G.

269–70. *goldsmiths' wives...rings* Cf. *M. of V.* 5. 1. 148–51.

269–70. *conned them* F. 'cond the'

271. *answer you right painted cloth* Cf. note ll. 212–13 above and G. 'painted cloth.' The reference is to the trite verses or mottoes with which these cloths were adorned.

292. S.D. F. gives no 'exit.'

301. *sighing every minute and groaning every hour* Cf. *R. II*, 5. 5. 50–60. The two passages would seem to be suggested by some common original wherein human nature and the clock were compared.

310. *trots hard* i.e. trots with uneasy pace. Cf. *Ado*, 2. 1. 334 'Time goes on crutches till love have all his rites.' v. G. 'hard.'

324. *go as softly* i.e. walk as slowly. Cf. *Ham.* 4. 4. 8 'Go softly on.'

334. *the cony that you see* A pretty piece of scene-painting; the rabbits are about them as they talk.

339. *religious* v. G. The idea Rosalind wishes to convey is that of some kind of hermit. This imaginary uncle apparently becomes the magician of 5. 4. 33.

340. *courtship* with a quibble upon life at 'court.'

341. *well, for* F. 'well: for'

342. *lectures* F. 'Lectors'

355. *deifying* (F2) F. 'defying' *Rosalind:* F. 'Roſalinde.'

359. *love-shaked* v. G. 'quotidian' and *Hen. V*, 2. 1. 124.

363. *you are* F. 'you art'

365–66. *a blue eye* v. G.

370–73. *Then your hose...careless desolation* Cf. *Ham.* 2. 1. 78–80.

374. *accoutrements* F. 'accouſtrements'

391. *a dark house and a whip* Cf. the treatment of Malvolio in *Tw. Nt.*

397. *manner.* So F.

399. *woo me: at* F. 'woe me At'

408. *a living humour of madness* Johnson suggested

'loving' for 'living' and many edd. agree; but v. G. 'living.'

411. *liver* regarded at this period as the seat of the passions.

424. S.D. F. 'Exeunt.'

3. 3.

S.D. F. 'Enter Clowne, Audrey, & Iaques:'

4. *features* This has puzzled many; but v. G.

7. *capricious* The learned Touchstone quibbles upon the etymological meaning of the word (viz. 'goat-like'), just as he puns upon 'goats' and 'Goths.' *honest Ovid* is an excellent description of the author of the *Ars amandi*; 'honest,' of course, meaning 'chaste.'

8–9. *Jove in a thatched house* alluding to the story of Baucis and Philemon; cf. *Ado*, G. 'Philemon.'

10–13. *When a man's verses...it strikes a man more dead...in a little room.* Cf. pp. 104–105.

12. *understanding,* F. 'underſtanding:'

18. *feigning;* F. 'faining,'

19. *it may be said* (Mason) F. 'may be ſaid' The omission of little words like 'it' is so common in F., and the addition of 'it' here renders so lucid what most agree with Dr Johnson is 'perplexed and inconsequent' as it stands, that we cannot doubt Mason to be right.

29. *material* v. G.

40. *Sir Oliver Martext* v. p. 105 and G. 'Sir.'

47. *horn-beasts.* So F.

49. *necessary.* So F.

51. *them.* So F.

dowry i.e. what his wife brings him.

52–3. *Horns? Even so. Poor men alone?* (Theobald) F. 'hornes, euen ſo poore men alone:' Theobald's reading is only a makeshift, and it seems highly probable that the compositor omitted a line of MS in setting up his type at the foot of the column.

54. *rascal* v. G.

59. *want* i.e. want one.

S.D. F. 'Enter Sir Oliuer Mar-text.'

61. *met.* So F.

68. *Proceed* etc. Jaques' alacrity is entertaining: he doffs his hat because he imagines that the marriage-service is about to begin. Touchstone (l. 73) takes it as an act of courtesy to Audrey and himself, and condescendingly desires him to 'be covered,' as if he were an Elizabethan nobleman and Jaques his inferior. Cf. note 5. 1. 17 below, *M.N.D.* 4. 1. 20 (note), *L.L.L.* 5. 1. 95, and *Ham.* 5. 2. 108.

70. *Master What-ye-call't* Touchstone deliberately leaves it doubtful whether he has forgotten the name of Jaques or is too refined a gentleman to mention it in the presence of a lady. Cf. *Characters in the Play,* p. 110.

71. *God'ild you* v. G. It may be significant that Touchstone twice employs this somewhat old-fashioned expression, which perhaps sounded a little affected in Shakespeare's day.

73. *pray be covered* See note l. 68 above.

75. *his bow* i.e. his yoke. v. G.

76. *desires;* F. 'deſires,'

80. *a good priest* It is evident from this that Jaques did not regard Martext as a real priest; he took him, we suppose, to be a Puritan preacher; cf. p. 105.

83. *warp* v. G. Jaques quibbles.

88. *Go thou with me* etc. F. divides 'Go thou with me,/And let me counsel thee' as if it were verse; and as a matter of fact 'And let me counsel thee' would serve as the half-line necessary to complete Touchstone's rhymed couplet. Clearly we have here a trace of the unrevised text; cf. pp. 94–8. It is noteworthy that everywhere else in the scene Jaques addresses Touchstone as 'you.'

89. *Come, sweet Audrey* F. heads this 'Ol.' in error.

90. *We must be married* i.e. properly in church.

91. *Farewell, good Master Oliver* etc. F. prints this as prose, and it may have been added to the end of the original scene. Note (i) Touchstone's Audrey-bawdry couplet brings the scene to a natural close; (ii) Touchstone's bamboozling of Sir Oliver with his dance-song is so similar to the treatment of Malvolio by the Clown in *Tw. Nt.* at the end of 4. 2. that the two incidents must surely have been penned approximately at the same time—possibly for Armin who succeeded Kempe as the clown of Shakespeare's Company about 1599. Touchstone evidently quotes from a well-known ballad. Steevens notes that 'O brave Oliver, leave me not behind you' is a quotation at the beginning of one of Breton's letters in his *Poste with a Packet of Mad Letters*, 1600, and that a ballad with much the same title was entered in the Stationers' Register to Richard Jones on 6 August 1584. Capell suggested that the fool dances about Sir Oliver 'with harlequin gesture and action' as he sings the stanzas.

100. S.D. F. 'Exeunt.'

3. 4.

S.D. F. 'Enter Rofalind & Celia.'

1–14. *Never talk* etc. F. for some reason breaks up this prose into short lengths. This has of course nothing whatever to do with any possible verse-original beneath the prose of this scene, of which indeed we have found no traces. Cf. 2. 6. head-note.

7. *the dissembling colour* The hair of Judas was traditionally red in colour.

14. *holy bread* v. G.

15. *cast* i.e. cast off, discarded. F2 and many edd. read 'chaste', and Furness ridicules 'cast' as absurd; but is there anything more ludicrous in supposing that Diana discarded a pair of lips than in declaring that Orlando 'bought' them? Celia is gently railing as usual, of course.

24. *covered goblet* v. G.

29. *a lover* (F2) F. 'Louer'

33. *I met the duke yesterday* 'Rosalind is not a very dutiful daughter, but her neglecting so long to make herself known to her father, though not quite proper, is natural enough. She cannot but be aware that in her disguise she is acting a perilous and not very delicate part, which is yet so delightful that she cannot prevail on herself to forego it, as her father would certainly have commanded her to do' (Hartley Coleridge). This piece of criticism is worth perpetuating as a specimen of early 19th cent. propriety. Shakespeare of course thought of none of these matters. His interest in the story is but fitful in this play, at any rate when making his final draft; but it flickers up for a moment here and so gives us this little passage about the Duke, which it will be noticed is entirely parenthetical and bears no relation either to what precedes or to what follows.

34. *question* v. G.

39–41. *breaks them...quite traverse...as a puisne tilter* 'like an unskilful tilter, who breaks his lance across instead of striking it full against his adversary's shield and so splitting it lengthways' (Wright). Cf. G. 'puisne,' *Ado*, 5. 1. 136, and *All's Well*, 2. 1. 70.

42. *a noble goose* The word 'goose' is pointless, or at any rate very weak, and many have suspected corruption. We suggest that Shakespeare may have written 'gofe' or 'goofe' which would be easily misread as 'gose' or 'goose'. N.E.D. gives 16th and 17th cent. examples of 'goff' meaning an awkward or stupid fellow, and connects it with the Fr. 'goffe' (=awkward, stupid). The emendation introduces the idea of gawkiness which the context requires.

43. S.D. F. 'Enter Corin.'

50. *the pale complexion of true love* alluding to the idea that 'With sighs of love that costs the fresh blood dear' the lover grows 'pale of cheer' (*M.N.D.* 3. 2. 97).

56. S.D. F. 'Exeunt.'

3. 5.

S.D. F. 'Enter Siluius and Phebe.'

1. *not, Phebe:* F. 'not Phebe'

7. *dies and lives.* Arrowsmith, quoting parallels from *The Romaunt of the Rose* and Barclay's *Ship of Fooles* (1570), has shown that 'this *hysteron proteron* is by no means uncommon: its meaning is of course the same as "live and die" i.e. subsist from the cradle to the grave.' Nevertheless, we think the inversion more likely to be due to inadvertence on the part of the compositor than to deliberation on that of Shakespeare.

S.D. F. 'Enter Rofalind, Celia, and Corin.'

12–13. *That eyes...atomies* This surely comes from the same corner of Shakespeare's brain as *L.L.L.* 4. 3. 334–5 'more soft and sensible/Than are the tender horns of cockled snails.'

22. *lean but upon* (F2) F. 'Leane vpon'

23. *capable impressure* i.e. sensible impression.

27. short line. Has Shakespeare cancelled some passage here in revision?   29. *fancy* v. G.

36. *and all at once* i.e. and that too all in a breath (Steevens).

37. *you have no beauty* This has puzzled critics, many of whom have suggested emendations. Rosalind is of course sarcastic.

39. *Than without candle* etc. Furness compares the Fr. proverb 'Dans la nuit tous les chats sont gris.'

46–7. *inky brows...black silk hair...bugle eye-balls ...cheek of cream* Cf. *L.L.L.* 3. 1. 195–96

> A whitely wanton with a velvet brow,
> With two pitch-balls stuck in her face for eyes.

50. *foggy south* i.e. the south wind, or rather the south-west wind (v. N.E.D. 'south' B5). Cf. *Rom.* 1. 4. 103 'the dew-dropping south.'

52. *woman:* F. 'woman.'

62. *Foul is most foul, being foul* etc. Warburton, who declared this line absurd as it stands, proposed

'found' for the third 'foul'. The emendation seems to us attractive, and presents no difficulty graphically, 'founde' being misread as 'foule' or 'fowle'; cf. note 1. 3. 9, Sh. Hand, p. 94, and Ham, Sp. and Misp. p. 45.

66–9. *He's fallen in love* etc. The humour of this speech lies in the stage-situation. Phebe and Silvius are kneeling with clasped hands on either side of Rosalind, and she turns from one to the other as she speaks. Textually the lines are interesting as being the only piece of prose in a verse-scene and a passage which could be omitted without loss to the context.

68. *anger.* So F.

78–9. *though all the world could see* etc. 'though all mankind could look on you none would be so deceived as to think you beautiful but he' (Dr Johnson).

80. S.D. F. 'Exit.'

81–2. *Dead Shepherd* etc. See pp. 103–104 for observations upon this famous reference to Marlowe. Cf. *Summer's Last Will*, ll. 1172–3 (McKerrow's *Nashe*, iii, 271):

Well sung a shepheard (that now sleepes in skies)
Dumme swannes do loue, & not vaine chattering pies;

which refers to Sidney, *Ast. & Stella*, Son. 54:

Dumb swans, not chattering pies, do lovers prove.

90. *Thou hast my love—is not that neighbourly?* This has so far been little commented upon, yet the sense is hardly clear at first sight. The point of the speech, we take it, is the last word; 'neighbourly' love being at this period commonly distinguished from 'conjugal' love (N.E.D. quotes from 1626 'it must be onely with neighbourly and ciuill, not with a conjugal love'). Phebe is still teasing Silvius: 'Thou hast my love,' she concedes, but takes back her words at once in what follows.

92. *Silvius*, F. 'Siluius;'

92. *thee*, F. 'thee;' 93. *love;* F. 'loue,'—transposed pointing.

100. *in such a poverty of grace* because his divinity has been so ungracious to him.

105. *erewhile* F. 'yere-while'

107. *bounds* i.e. 'bounds of feed' (2. 4. 80).

123. *mingled damask* i.e. red and white like damask roses; cf. G. 'damask' and *Son.* 130. 5, 6

> I have seen roses damasked red and white
> But no such roses see I in her cheeks.

128. *I have* (F2) F. 'Haue'

132. *again:* F. 'againe,'

139. S.D. F. 'Exeunt.'

4. I.

S.D. F. 'Enter Rosalind, and Celia, and Iaques.'

1. *let me be better* (F2) F. 'let me better'

3. *They say* etc. A line of blank verse.

5. *Those that are in extremity of either* Cf. *M. of V.* I. I. 51–6.

6. *abominable* F. 'abhominable'—the usual spelling. Clearly the word is here used with a suggestion of the false etymology *ab homine* in which everyone believed at this period.

6–7. *betray themselves...worse than drunkards* This has puzzled some, probably because our manners are different from those of Shakespeare's day when the sight of a helpless drunkard in the streets, exposed to the jeers and practical jokes of any passer-by, must have been a common one.

to every modern censure i.e. to the criticism of every normal individual. v. G. 'modern.'

10–19. *I have neither...humorous sadness* Maginn (1860) declared this speech to be in blank verse and attempted to rearrange accordingly. The result made what Furness rightly calls 'rather ragged verse.' Yet it can hardly be doubted that the speech was once verse, which Shakespeare has re-written as prose, the most obvious indication of this being the last few lines which with the opening words of Rosalind's rejoinder, if the slight change from 'By my faith' to 'I'faith' be allowed, make excellent and indubitable verse. Thus:

> The sundry contemplation of my travels,
> In which my often rumination wraps me
> In a most humorous sadness.
> *Ros.*   A traveller!
> I'faith, you have great reason to be sad.

Jaques' gibe at blank verse (l. 29) makes it quite certain, of course, that Shakespeare deliberately converted the verse into prose. Cf. pp. 94–8.

10. *the scholar's melancholy, which is emulation* A melancholy comment upon much Shakespearian commentary.

18. *my often* (F2) F. 'by often'

24. S.D. F. 'Enter Orlando.'

28. S.D. It is clear that Rosalind ignores him at first in order to punish him for his tardiness (Grant White).

31–2. *look you lisp* etc. Cf. Howell, *Instructions for forreine travell* (1642): 'Foreign travel oftentimes makes many to wander from themselves as well as from their country, and to come back mere mimics....They strive to degenerate as much as they can from Englishmen, and all their talk is still foreign, or at least, will bring it to be so, though it be by head and shoulders, magnifying other nations and derogating from their own.' The extravagances of travellers was of course a common theme from the attack on the 'Englishman Italianate' in Ascham's *Schoolemàster* (1570) onwards.

36. *gondola* F. 'Gundello'

S.D. Most mod. edd. follow F2 and give Jaques his exit at l. 30, thus absurdly allowing Rosalind to apostrophise 'Monsieur Traveller' after he has left the stage. F. gives him no exit.

44. *thousandth* (Rowe) F. 'thouſand' The *th*

termination for the ordinal is not found before the 16th cent.

46. *clapped him o'th' shoulder* v. G.

59. *in his fortune* i.e. with the horns which it is his fate to earn.

prevents=anticipates.

73. *God warr'nt us* (Anon. *apud* Clark and Wright) F. 'God warne vs' Cf. *M.N.D.* 5. 1. 319 'God warnd vs' and *Ham.* 1. 2.243 'I warn't it will.' Onions (*Shak. Gloss.*) quoting the present passage and that from *M.N.D.* describes 'warn' as a wide-spread dialect pronunciation of 'warrant', but the *Ham.* example seems to suggest that 'warnt' or 'warnd' was the Shakespearian form, of which 'warne' in the present instance was merely a misprint.

84. *suit* This word which begins a new line in F. is left in the line by itself, 'Am not I your Rosalind?' being carried on to the next line. Were some words cut out of the text here?

95. *love: Leander* F. 'loue. Leander'

97. *nun, if* F. 'Nun; if'

100. *chroniclers* F. 'Chronoclers' Hanmer read 'coroners' and some of the foolish editors of this age have followed him.

133. *ask you for your commission* ask you what authority you have for taking her seeing that there is no one to give her away.

134–35. *There's a girl goes before the priest* Rosalind refers of course to her anticipation of what Celia ought to have said, but the expression has a proverbial ring, and probably contains some secondary meaning.

145. *a Barbary cock-pigeon* the Othello among pigeons. v. G.

146. *against rain* i.e. when the rain is coming on.

147. *new-fangled* v. G.

148–49. *like Diana in the fountain* i.e. the fickle hero of *Diana Enamorada* by Jorge de Montemayor, a long pastoral romance. An Eng. trans. by Bartholomew Young, pub. 1598 but stated in Preface to have been in MS for sixteen years, may have been known to Sh. The romance opens with an account by one of her lovers of Diana swearing eternal fidelity to him while she shed tears 'like orient pearls' into the fountain by which she sat. Young dedicated his book to his 'very good Lady the Lady Rich'.

161. *Wit, whither wilt?* an Elizabethan phrase commonly addressed to foolish prattlers. Cf. note I. 2. 52.

169. *her husband's occasion* i.e. a handle against her husband; v. G. 'occasion.'

180. *'tis but one cast away, and so, come death* This seems to Furness 'like some quotation or allusion whose popularity excuses, or at least lightens, the charming exaggeration.'

184. *all pretty oaths that are not dangerous* Cf. I *Hen. IV*, 3. 1. 253–55. Some have supposed this to be a reference to the statute against blasphemy on the stage passed in 1605, and that it is accordingly a late insertion.

187. *pathetical break-promise* v. G. In 'hollow lover' Rosalind repeats the same idea reversed so to speak. It is noteworthy that Shakespeare only uses 'pathetical'—a favourite word with Nashe—here and in *L.L.L.* (v. G.). Cf. pp. 105–107.

195. S.D. F. 'Exit.'

196. *simply misused* absolutely slandered.

197–99. Steevens notes the closeness of this to Lodge's original: 'And I pray you (quoth Aliena), if your robes were off, what mettall are you made of that you are so satyricall against woman? is it not a foule bird defiles his own nest?'

203. *the bay of Portugal* 'still used by sailors to denote that portion of the sea off the coast of Portugal from Oporto to the headland of Cintra' (Wright).

205. *in, it* (F2) F. 'in, in'

211. *shadow* i.e. shady spot.
213. S.D. F. 'Exeunt.'

4. 2.

S.D. F. 'Enter Iaques and Lords, Forresters.' We take 'Forresters' as a costume-direction, in apposition to 'Lords'; cf. S.D. 2. 1. head. An entry is given to Amiens, because being the singer of the company the actor who plays him would be needed for the song (v. Richmond Noble, *Shakespeare's Use of Song*, p. 77).

This short scene is one full of difficulty for an editor. First of all, what exactly is supposed to be happening? It is clear, we think, that Jaques has just encountered a party of lords returning from a deer-hunt, ending in a kill. They are elated with their success, and Jaques, delighting as ever to foster human folly, eggs them on to the top of their bent. There shall be a procession in which the deer-slayer shall be borne in triumph, like a Roman conqueror, to the Duke's presence: it will be fitting also that he wear the deer's horns and skin, as the insignia of victory. In all this, we do not doubt, Shakespeare had in mind folk-customs connected with the hunt and going back to the days of pre-Christian sacrifice which are now lost in oblivion (for the wearing of heads and skins of animals cf. Chambers, *Mediaeval Stage*, i. 166, 258, who strangely enough makes no reference to this scene). Moreover, if we may judge from the horned Falstaff in *M.W.W.* and the hunting-scene in Munday's *Death of Robert Earl of Huntingdon* (1598) which introduces 'Frier Tuck carrying a stags head dauncing,' stags' heads were for some reason popular on the stage at this time. In any event it is obvious that the decking of the victor in the victim's horns and hide, the hoisting of him upon the shoulders of his fellows and the bearing him 'home' to the Duke with boisterous song and triumph formed the staple of this scene, in which action is far more important than dialogue, and which with its riotous character and traditional appeal would be very popular with an Elizabethan audience. We have arranged the scene accordingly, placing it 'before the cave of the exiled Duke,' since the words 'present him to the duke' and 'sing him home' suggest such a venue. No trace of the deer, of course, except the horns and hide would appear on the stage.

7. *Amiens*. F. heads this 'Lord' Rowe reads 'For.' (=forester) and many mod. edd. follow him.

8–9. *no matter...noise enough* Amiens would be a trained singer but the chorus was composed of ordinary players. Thus Shakespeare apologises for their vocal deficiencies.

10–19. The Song. As the arrangement of this song has been much debated by editors, it will be well to give the F. text exactly.

Muſicke, Song.

What ſhall he haue that kild the Deare?
His Leather skin, and hornes to weare:
Then ſing him home, the reſt ſhall beare this burthen;
Take thou no ſcorne to weare the horne,
It was a creſt ere thou waſt borne,
Thy fathers father wore it,
And thy father bore it,
The horne, the horne, the luſty horne,
Is not a thing to laugh to ſcorne.

The main difficulty lies in the third line. Since the time of Theobald most have agreed that the words 'the rest shall beare this burthen' form a S.D., and that 'Then sing him home' is the 'burthen' which 'the rest' are to 'bear.' A few, however, viz. Knight, Collier, Grant White, Dyce and Hudson, consider that the line hangs together and was intended to be taken as a single S.D. Our own reading involves no tampering with the F. text beyond the carry-over of the two last words of the line,

which reveals a third rhyme to 'deer' and 'wear.' The
arrangement finds a close parallel in *Temp.* 1.2.380–82:

> Foot it featly here and there,
> And sweet sprites bear
> The burthen...

19. S.D. F. 'Exeunt.'

4. 3.

S.D. F. 'Enter Roſalind and Celia.'
1–5. F. prints this prose as verse, and Walker even
supposed that Shakespeare intended it as such. If we
preserve the F. lining and make use of square brackets
to pick out the prose, we get this:

> *Ros.* How say you now, is it not past two o'clock?
> [And here much Orlando.]
>   *Cel.* I warr'nt you, with pure love and troubled brain,
> He hath ta'en his bow and arrows and [is] gone forth
> To sleep: [look, who comes here.]
>   *Sil.* My errand is to you, fair youth.

On our theory of the text, it is clear that the dialogue
between Rosalind and Celia before the entrance of
Silvius originally consisted of verse which ran to more
than five lines and that Shakespeare in revising cut it
down and converted it into prose in the process. The
addition of two pieces of prose, 'And here much Orlando' and 'look, who comes here', which no doubt
took the place of deleted passages, was enough by itself
to turn the whole into prose. The reference to Orlando's
'bow and arrows' is a little mysterious and may have
been more explicit in the first draft.

5. S.D. F. 'Enter Siluius'—after l. 3.
7. *bid* (F2) F. 'did bid' All edd. follow F2 and
we do likewise, though with some hesitation, seeing that
a similar emendation is necessary at 5. 4. 21 (q.v.) in
order to preserve the dissyllabic pronunciation of Phebe.
23. *turned into* brought into. Aldis Wright com-

pares *Temp.* 1. 2. 64, *Two Gent.* 4. 4. 59, *Tw. Nt.* 2. 5. 224, *Cor.* 3. 1. 284. *love.* So F.

48. *vengeance* v. G.

58. *seal up thy mind* make thy final decision. v. G. 'seal up.'

74. S.D. F. 'Exit. Sil.'/'Enter Oliuer.'

75. *fair ones* 'Shakespeare seems to have forgotten that Celia was apparently the only woman present' (Aldis Wright). Is there any reason why Oliver, a man of middle age, should not address 'the boy' and his 'sister' as 'fair ones'? He had been told, 'the boy is fair.'

87. *a ripe forester* F. 'a ripe ſiſter' Lettsom suggested 'a right forester', pointing out that 'forester' was often written 'forster' or 'foster', and both Dyce and Furness approved, the latter justly remarking that 'ripe sister' as applied to Ganymede is an expression 'not merely odd but almost unintelligible.' Lettsom, we think, was right about 'forester' which in the form 'foster' might easily be misread as 'ſiſter', while the change provides the extra syllable required by the metre. But 'right' is quite unnecessary, for 'bestows himself like a ripe forester' (i.e. conducts himself like an experienced forester) is a description most applicable to Ganymede with his 'swashing and a martial outside,' his 'gallant curtle-axe,' and his 'boar-spear' (1. 3. 117–20).

104. *an oak* (Pope) F. 'an old Oake' The change, essential to the metre, is accepted by all.

105. *antiquity,* F. 'antiquitie:'

113. *bush:* F. 'buſh,'

118. *To prey...dead* A very old notion, found in Pliny, and widely current in Renaissance times.

123. *livèd* F. 'liu'd'

129. *his just occasion* his perfectly legitimate excuse (for refusing to help his brother).

130. *lioness,* F. 'Lyonneſſe:'

131. *before him:* F. 'before him,'

141. *As how...place* As Capell notes 'other heads of these brothers' "recountments" are apparently necessary to make the Poet's "in brief" right and sensible.' Malone suggested that a line has been lost.

142. *In brief* (F2) F. 'I briefe'

155. *his blood* (F2) F. 'this bloud' The 'his' is so much the better that we cannot doubt it to be Shakespeare's. Probably the compositor's eye was misled by 'this' later in the line.

159. *Cousin, Ganymede!* F. 'Cofen Ganimed. Dr Johnson, who reads 'Cousin—Ganymed!', comments: 'Celia in her first fright, forgets Rosalind's character and disguise, and calls out "cousin," then recollects herself, and says, "Ganymede".'

160–67. *Look, he recovers* etc. We follow the F. lining here exactly, which shows an interesting mixture of prose and verse. Cf. pp. 94–8.

181. S.D. F. 'Exeunt.'

5. 1.

S.D. F. 'Enter Clowne and Awdrie.'

4. *old gentleman's* an interesting piece of evidence on the age of Jaques.

9. S.D. F. 'Enter William.'

10. *clown* i.e. country rustic. The humour of this scene lies in the assertion by Touchstone of the mental and moral superiority of the court clown over the country clown. He browbeats William with phrases and preserves throughout an air of ineffable hauteur. William, of course, grows more and more dumbfounded as the scene proceeds.

12. *we shall...hold* i.e. we must have our jest; we cannot help ourselves.

14. *God ye good ev'n* One of the many forms of 'God give you good even.'

17. *friend.* So F. *cover thy head* This act of

condescension, which Touchstone had already tried with Jaques (cf. 3. 3. 68 note), at once places him in the position of a gentleman talking to an inferior.

36–7. *when he put it into his mouth* These, we take it, are the emphatic words. Touchstone affects to suppose hat William has his mouth open to swallow up Audrey, and tells him that the grape is not yet in it.

39. *sir* (F2) F. 'ſit'

42. *have;* F. 'haue.'

45. *other;* F. 'other.'

49–59. *Therefore, you clown* etc. This passage is strongly reminiscent of Armado's epistolary style in *L.L.L.* The courtly jargon which is serious with Armado is mocked at by Touchstone. It has been necessary to modernise the punctuation of this speech rather drastically.

58. *policy* (F2) F. 'police'

61. S.D. F. 'Exit.'/'Enter Corin.'

62. *seek* (Rowe) F. 'ſeekes'

65. S.D. F. 'Exeunt.'

5. 2.

S.D. F. 'Enter Orlando & Oliuer.'

1–18. For the traces of verse beneath this prose, v. pp. 94–5.

5. *question,* F. 'queſtion;'

7. *nor her* (Rowe) F. 'nor'

12. S.D. F. 'Enter Roſalind.'

13–16. This speech is printed as verse in F. and was undoubtedly intended to be so originally. Cf. pp. 94–5.

18. *fair sister* Orlando has just spoken of Ganymede as 'my Rosalind,' and Oliver, about to marry the sister of this 'Rosalind,' quite naturally calls 'him' in jest his 'sister.' If you are Orlando's Rosalind, he implies, you are my sister.

20. *wear thy heart in a scarf* Orlando has worn his

heart on his sleeve ever since he entered the forest, and now his arm is wounded Rosalind calls it his heart.

30. *Cæsar's thrasonical brag* The thrasonical Armado quotes the brag in *L.L.L.* 4. 1. 67. The word 'thrasonical,' a favourite expression with Nashe, only occurs in these two plays of Shakespeare.

31. *overcame* (F2) F. 'ouercome'

35-6. *in these degrees...a pair of stairs* a quibble, 'degree' still retaining something of its original meaning of 'step.' Cf. *Jul. Cæs.* 2. 1. 25-7 'He then unto the ladder turns his back...scorning the base degrees by which he did ascend.' v. G. 'pair of stairs.'

39. *clubs cannot part them* The allusion is to the cry of 'Clubs!' raised in the London streets when any brawl was toward, ostensibly to summon the citizens to *part* the combatants. Rosalind is carrying on the idea of 'the wrath of love.'

50-71. *Know of me* etc. It is noteworthy that the whole style of the prose changes at this point, and gives us a stilted dialogue strongly reminiscent of the stilted prose in *Measure* (v. pp. xxxvii–xxxix). How ludicrous, for instance, seems it that Rosalind should suddenly assure Orlando that he is 'a gentleman of good conceit.' The purpose of the dialogue here is to prepare Orlando and the audience for the Hymen masque in 5. 4. Now if, as we suspect, this masque was a substitution by another dramatist for a different solution provided by Shakespeare, the re-writing of the dialogue here would be explained.

53. *insomuch* = inasmuch as. The F. punctuation 'knowledge: infomuch (I fay) I know' etc. shows the compositor has misunderstood the sense.

60. *out,* F. 'out:'

61. *her.* So F.

64-5. *human...danger* 'that is, not a phantom but the real Rosalind, without any of the danger generally conceived to attend the rites of incantation' (Dr Johnson).

67–8. *I tender dearly ... magician* Supposedly a reference to the statutes against witchcraft, i.e. 5 Eliz. ch. 16, 'An Act agaynst Coniuracons, Inchantmentes, and Witchcraftes,' which enumerated various penalties against wizardry according to the gravity of the offence. But a much severer act passed in the first year of James's reign really made the profession of magician a dangerous one, since anyone invoking or consulting with evil spirits and practising witchcraft was to be put to death. If we could suppose that this portion of the text of *As You Like It* was of Jacobean origin, Rosalind's words would gain great point.

71. S.D. F. 'Enter Siluius & Phebe.'

78. A strong accent upon both 'him's' alone makes this line metrical.

92–4. *obedience* (Malone) F. 'observance'. The compositor has inadvertently repeated at the end of l. 94 the word he has already set up at the end of l. 92. Many conjectures have been made, e.g. 'obedience', 'endurance', 'obeisance', 'deservance'—all pure guesswork.

102. *Who..to* (Rowe) F. 'Why...too'

104–105. *the howling of Irish wolves against the Moon* Cf. *M.N.D.* 5. 1. 370 'And the wolf behowls the moon.' The reference is, of course, to monotonous cries repeated ad nauseam; but why 'Irish' wolves especially? We suggest that there is here a reference to the Irish rebellion of 1598 and the campaign under the Earl of Essex which followed. Irish rebels rising against the Virgin Queen, the English Diana, might be aptly compared with wolves howling against the moon. Sh. Eng. (i. 519) refers to the notion recorded by Spenser that the Irish 'were once every year turned into wolves.'

119. S.D. F. 'Exeunt.'

5.3.

S.D. F. 'Enter Clowne and Audrey.'

This scene 'was evidently added—it has no bearing whatever on the development of the action,' and was probably 'specially devised to meet the growing taste for song and possibly to counter the attractions of the Children at Blackfriars, where there were the best trained choristers the metropolis possessed' (R. Noble, *Shakespeare's Use of Song*, p. 76).

4. *dishonest* immodest. *a woman of the world* a married woman. Cf. *Ado*, 2. 1. 298.

9. *sit i'th' middle* Roffe (*Musical Triad*, 1872) plausibly suggests that Touchstone is to sit i'th' middle in order that he may take part in the song, and that he joined in the lines common to all the stanzas.

13. *both in a tune* Mr Noble infers from this 'that the boys sing in unison' (*op. cit.* p. 75). Cowden-Clarke, on the other hand, took it as equivalent to 'in time.'

14. *gipsies* One of those little touches of local colour of which this play is full. Cf. note 2. 5. 52.

15. *It was a lover* etc. Chappell (*Popular Music of the Olden Time*) printed a version of this song, with a 17th cent. setting, which he discovered in MS at the Advocates' Library, Edinburgh. In some ways this text is more correct than that of the F., e.g. F. prints the last stanza after the first and gives us 'rang time' for 'ring time'. Other interesting variants are also noted. P.S. 1947:—The Edinburgh MS was taken from Morley's *First Book of Airs*, 1600, a unique copy of which, now in the Folger Library, Washington, was reprinted in 1932 by Canon Fellowes (Stainer & Bell, Ltd.), who believes that Sh. did not write the song but borrowed it from Morley; see also his letter *T.L.S.* 5 Jan. 1933.

16. *nonino:* F. 'nonino,' But F. reads 'nonino:' in all the other stanzas.

18. *In spring time* (Edinburgh MS) F. 'In the spring time' As F. reads 'In spring time' at the end of

the other stanzas, we may take 'the' to be a misprint here.

ring time (Edinburgh MS) F. 'rang time'—a minim error.

21. F. here reads the stanza beginning 'And therefore take' etc., with which the song should obviously conclude, as it does in the Edin. MS. How came the stanzas to be disarranged in F.? Possibly the first and last stanzas in the original MS were given with the music and the other two stanzas written separately.

Between the acres of the rye Ridgeway suggests that here we have a reference to the grass baulks which divided the corn-fields into strips under the old system of open-field cultivation.

23. *folks would* Edin. MS reads 'fools did' which seems to us an improvement.

27. *carol* v. G.

29. *life* (Edin. MS) F. 'a life' Cf. *Job* xiv. 2 and 1 *Pet.* i. 24.

33. *And therefore...time* Edin. MS reads 'Then prettie louers take the tyme'

35. *prime* v. G. Cf. *Son.* 3. 9–10.

41. *untuneable* i.e. discordant, not in tune. Touchstone is not criticising the setting but the rendering, in which the 'time' was all-important. The reply of the pages is therefore quite to the point.

46. S.D. F. 'Exeunt.'

5. 4.

S.D. F. 'Enter Duke Senior, Amyens, Iaques, Orlando, Oliuer, Celia.' N.B. Amiens is given nothing to say in the scene as it stands. Cf. note l. 105 below.

4. *that fear they hope, and know they fear* The sense is not in doubt, but the phrasing is doubtful, and many emendations have been proposed, the simplest and most satisfactory being Heath's 'that fear their hope and

know their fear'. The words 'their' and 'they' might easily be confused.

S.D. F. 'Enter Roſalinde, Siluius, & Phebe.'

18–25. *to make all this matter even...To make these doubts all even* This kind of clumsy repetition is unusual with Shakespeare. The expression 'made even' recurs in Hymen's song l. 106 below. Cf. *Measure*, 3. 1. 40–1 'Yet death we fear,/That makes these odds all even.'

21. *Keep your word, Phebe* (Rowe) F. 'Keepe you your word Phebe' Cf. note 4. 3. 7. The only way of scanning the F. line is to take Phebe as a monosyllable; on the other hand, with 'Keep you your word' (l. 19) and 'You yours' (l. 20) the compositor would be tempted to set up 'you your' once again.

25. short line, but of no textual significance.

S.D. F. 'Exit Roſ. and Celia.'

34. *Obſcuréd...forest* Alluding perhaps to the magic circle within which a wizard was safe from devils.

S.D. F. 'Enter Clowne and Audrey.'—after l. 33.

36. *ark.* So F.

42–3. *put me to my purgation* The quibble recurs in *Ham.* 'put him to his purgation' (3. 2. 318).

47. *ta'en up* v. G. 'take up.'

53. *I desire you of the like* i.e. may you remain in that frame of mind.

59. *honesty* i.e. chastity.

62. *swift and sententious* prompt and pithy.

63–4. *According...diseases* Cf. *M. of V.* 2. 2. 58 'according to fates and destinies, and such odd sayings, the sisters three, and such branches of learning.' That two clowns so different as Lancelot and Touchstone should employ the same turn of phrase suggests that it may have been some catch expression of the day. 'The fool's bolt' refers of course to the proverb 'a fool's bolt is soon shot,' but no one has discovered the significance of 'dulcet diseases.'

65. *cause.* So F.

67. *seven times removed* Touchstone counts backwards from the 'lie direct.'

67–8. *removed...Audrey* F. 'remoued: (beare... Audry)'

68–9. *did dislike* i.e. expressed my dislike of.

71. *Courteous.* So F.   74. *Modest.* So F.

76. *Churlish.* So F.   78. *Valiant.* So F.

80. *so to the Lie* (F2) F. 'ſo ro lye'

88. *we quarrel in print* The quibble here seems to have been overlooked, 'in print' meaning 'with precision,' 'in exact order'; cf. *L.L.L.* 3. 1. 170.

by the book In 1594–5 appeared Vincentio Saviola's *Practise of the Rapier and Dagger*, dedicated to the Earl of Essex, and dealing among other matters pertaining to 'honour and honorable quarrels' with 'the manner and diversity of Lies,' which are classified as 'lies certain' and 'conditional lies.' This is the book to which Touchstone is supposed to be referring. Another possibility is *The Booke of Honor and Armes, wherein is discoursed the Causes of Quarrell, and the nature of Iniuries, with their Repulses* (1590) at which Shakespeare was certainly laughing in *L.L.L.* (v. note 1. 2. 170). But it is not necessary to attach Touchstone's words to any particular book; enough that such books existed and were known to exist by Shakespeare and his audience.

89. *books for good manners* alluding to the numerous 'courtesy books' of the period.

90. *degrees.* 95. *If.* 99. *brothers.* All F. periods.

103. *stalking-horse* v. G.

104. *presentation* v. G.

S.D. F. 'Enter Hymen, Roſalind, and Celia.'/'Still Muſicke.' Ben Jonson thus described the costume of Hymen in his *Hymenaei*: 'Hymen, the god of marriage, in a saffron coloured robe, his under vestures white, his sockes yellow, a yellow veile of silke on his left arme, his head crowned with roses and marjoram, in his right hand a torch of pine-tree.'

There is no dramatic necessity for this masque-business; the appearance of Hymen is completely unexpected, seeing that what we have been led to anticipate is a magician (5. 2. 58–68; 5. 4. 31–4); Hymen's words, whether spoken or sung, do not seem to us in the least Shakespearian; and they might all be omitted without loss to the context. In a word we regard the masque as a non-Shakespearian interpolation, probably added to the text in the reign of James I, when masques were very fashionable, in order to deck out the play for a wedding. Indeed, we think it likely that ll. 105–47 represent a page of MS written by the reviser to take the place of a magician-episode of the original. The octosyllabic couplets and the other rhyming couplets remind us, in their obscurity and tortuousness, of the verse of a similar kind in *Meas.*, which we attributed to a non-Shakespearian hand. Cf. *Meas.* pp. 110–11.

105. *Then is there mirth* etc. F. heads this simply 'Hymen'; but the S.D. 'Still Muficke' and the metrical scheme of the verse obviously suggest a song. The fact that Amiens is given an entry at the head of the scene in F. but has nothing to say or sing in the received text suggests that his original part was cut by the reviser in order that the actor who played him might come on as Hymen.

111. *her hand* (F3) F. 'his hand'

112. *her bosom* (Malone) F. 'his bofome' Edd. who adopt 'her' in l. 111 hesitate to make the same change here. If 'his bosom' be retained then the antecedent to 'whose' must be 'her hand' which is awkward. Malone's change removes all difficulty.

113. *yours.* So F.

127. *If truth holds true contents* The only point of this feeble line seems to be that it provides a rhyme for 'events.'

134. *we sing* The song that follows is therefore not a solo as before.

137. *and these things finish* Another very feeble phrase.

138–43. F. heads this 'Song' and prints in italics. The words 'we sing' (l. 134) indicate that more than one voice is required, while the matter is obviously one for a chorus. 'Both the thought and the form of the thought in this "Song" seem to me as unlike Shakespeare's as they could well be, and no less unworthy of his genius; and for the same reasons I think it not improbable that the whole of Hymen's part is from another pen than his' (Grant White).

141. *High* an adverb not an adjective.

145. *Even daughter* etc. Critics seem to agree that the Duke is here still addressing Celia and telling her that he welcomes her as a daughter; but how obscure and tortuous the language is! 'The rhyme,' as Verity puts it, 'accounts for the curious turn of the expression.' The language of ll. 146–47 is even more strained.

147. S.D. F. 'Enter Second Brother.' The speech is also headed '2. Bro.' The designation, borrowed probably from 'the second son' (l. 149), is clearly a part-name to distinguish this Jaques from the other. The name of this brother occurs only once in the play, at 1. 1. 5, and no one in the audience would be at all likely to remember it. We may indeed ask why the third De Boys should be dragged in here at all when a messenger would have done equally well; perhaps he played a more considerable part in the original draft.

153. *on foot* (F2) F. 'oh foote'—some copies (cf. Methuen facsimile).

157. *an old religious man* i.e. a hermit or monk. One wonders whether he once had something to do with Rosalind's imaginary uncle; cf. 5. 2. 58–68; 5. 4. 31–4.

158. *question* v. G. *converted* Such a conversion

was familiar to Shakespeare's generation in the person of Charles V.

161. *to them* (Rowe) F. 'to him'

164. *offer'st fairly* i.e. contributest handsomely.

166. *dukedom.* So F.   172. *states.* So F.

175. *music* i.e. musicians.

176. *measures* v. G.

177. *Sir, by your patience* A request to the Duke that the music should be stayed.

183. *bequeath* The word is appropriate to one taking his leave of the world.

184. *deserves it:* F. 'deſerues it.'

186. F. gives no indication to whom these various lines are addressed, but since the words 'true faith' can only apply to Orlando, the present line must refer to Oliver, who by marrying Celia had contracted 'great allies.'

193. S.D. F. 'Exit.'

194. *we will* (F2) F. 'wee'l'

195. S.D. F. 'Exit.' Capell first introduced the S.D. 'A dance' which all mod. edd. follow, no doubt correctly in view of ll. 175–76, 190. Cf. the conclusion of *Ado,* which belongs to the same period.

Epilogue. Not marked as such by F. as in other instances, but headed 'Roſ.' and printed continuously with the rest of the play. Can it have been transcribed for printing direct from her 'part'?

4. *epilogue:* F. 'Epilogue.'

10. *become me:* F. 'become mee.'

11. *women.* So F.

12–13. *to like as much of this play as please you* i.e. to like as much of it as it may please you to like. This is of course a reference to the title of the play.

15–16. *that between...please* There is of course a double meaning behind Rosalind's words. *please.* So F.

16. *If I were a woman* etc. The jest 'owes its point to the fact that it was delivered by a boy: on

the lips of an actress at the present day it has no meaning' (Mr Percy Simpson, Sh. Eng. ii. 247).

21. *bid me farewell* i.e. release me by your applause. Cf. *M.N.D.* Ep. 15 'Give me your hands, if we be friends,' and *Temp.* Ep. 9–10 'But release me from my bands,/With the help of your good hands.'

S.D. F. 'Exit.'

THE STAGE-HISTORY OF
AS YOU LIKE IT

On December 2, 1603, the King's Company was summoned from Mortlake to give a performance before King James I at the Earl of Pembroke's house at Wilton, where the Court, kept out of London by the plague, was then resident. There is, or was, a tradition in the Pembroke family that the play performed that day was *As You Like It* and that Shakespeare was one of the players. The only evidence suggested was a letter, said to be, or to have been, at Wilton, which no living eye has seen. (Lee, *A Life of William Shakespeare*, 1922, p. 691; and Chambers, *The Elizabethan Stage*, iii. 209.) Setting aside that tradition, there is no record of any performance of this play in the sixteenth and seventeenth centuries, although there is evidence (see above, p. 93) that in 1600 it was already popular. It was neglected by both Killigrew and D'Avenant after the Restoration, and it had to wait till 1740 for a hearing.

Before this hearing came, Charles Johnson had made free with parts of the play in concocting his *Love in a Forest*. This comedy, produced at Drury Lane in January 1723 and printed in the same year, has been mentioned in the stage-history of *A Midsummer-Night's Dream*, since the clowns with their Pyramus and Thisbe were brought in to entertain the banished Duke and his followers in the forest. Johnson made Charles and Orlando fight with rapiers and defy each other in language taken from Norfolk and Bolingbroke in the first act of *King Richard II*. He conceived, before George Sand, the notion of putting Jaques in love with Celia. That Colley Cibber, joint-manager of the theatre where *Love in a Forest* was produced, chose the part of Jaques may have been the cause or the effect of Johnson's enlargement of the part, which set a fashion long followed. Wilks played Orlando; Booth, the banished Duke; and

Mrs Booth, Rosalind. There was no Touchstone, and therefore no Audrey.

Professor Odell (*Shakespeare from Betterton to Irving*, i. 228) is disposed to attribute to Macklin the favour won for Shakespeare's romantic comedies in the third and fourth decades of the eighteenth century, when the earlier 'romantic movement' seemed to take advantage of the passing of Restoration comedy and of the great tragic actors. Macklin himself took no part in this first recorded production of Shakespeare's *As You Like It*. The theatre was Drury Lane; the date December 20, 1740. Quin played Jaques; Chapman, Touchstone; Milward, Orlando; Mrs Pritchard, Rosalind; and Mrs Clive, Celia. Dr Arne wrote the music for the songs; and the introduction of foreign dancers did not obscure the charm and beauty of Shakespeare's work. Ever since then the play has been in constant favour, both with the players and the playgoers; and its stage-history becomes a record of the changes in its cast. Macklin first appeared as Touchstone at Drury Lane in October 1741. Mrs Pritchard and Mrs Woffington were the rival Rosalinds from 1741 till 1750; and it was as Rosalind that Peg Woffington made her last appearance on the stage and her famous breakdown at Covent Garden on May 3, 1757. After her, all the leading actresses, and many who never led, tried the part. Among the best were Mrs Dancer (1767), who was held to be very good in it, Mrs Barry, Mrs Yates, Mrs Robinson and Mrs Wells. In April 1785 Mrs Siddons, taking her benefit at the Theatre Royal, essayed Rosalind for the first time. No matter what Boaden may say, the public felt, with Miss Seward, that 'the playful scintillations of colloquial wit, which most mark that character, suit not the dignity of the Siddonian countenance.' The public wanted a more bouncing Rosalind. And just two years later the public made acquaintance with the greatest Rosalind of them all, Mrs Jordan. From

April 1787 until 1814 Mrs Jordan went on playing Rosalind. And from October 1767 till 1802 King went on playing Touchstone. Other fine actors, Woodward, Shuter, Yates, Quick, Palmer, John Bannister, Suett, Dodd, Harley, did well in the part; but King, to his time's taste, was the perfect Touchstone. Among the Celias none could come up to Kitty Clive, who went on acting the part till 1763; but Mrs Baddeley, Mrs Mattocks, Mrs Mountain, Miss Mellon, Miss Brunton (who in 1817 also tried Rosalind and won no high praise for the effort from Hazlitt in *The Times*) and Miss Foote are in the long list. In the longer list of the players of Jaques are the names of Sparks, Aikin, Henderson, Palmer, Harley, John Philip Kemble and Macready.

For two hundred years after Charles Johnson the play was never badly mauled. Jaques's part was increased at the expense of the First Lord's, and this practice was continued through the managements of Garrick (who never acted in the piece himself) and of J. P. Kemble. There was some juggling, too, with the songs. The play's own songs, although there was Arne's music to sing them to, were cut out or cut down; and the very inappropriate 'Cuckoo Song' (which was 'When daisies pied' from *Love's Labour's Lost*) was regularly sung either by Celia or by Rosalind down to the eighteen-nineties (R. Noble, *Shakespeare's Use of Song*, 1923). Somehow *As You Like It* escaped Frederic Reynolds; but this juggling with the songs reached its worst in two operatic performances (apparently of two different versions) which were given at Covent Garden in 1824, with all Shakespeare's poems rifled for words to set to music. The composer of the second version was Bishop, and the Rosalind was Maria Tree. In 1825 at the Haymarket, Mme Vestris made her first appearance as Rosalind in yet another operatic version. These things were forgotten when Macready staged the play in 1837, and again, very beautifully, in 1842.

The increase in the number of London theatres after
1843 and the consequent, or subsequent, growth of a
new drama made no difference to the popularity of this
play on both sides of the curtain. Between Macready's
production and the present day it is hard to find a gap
of five years in its stage-history. In 1845 Helen Faucit
plays Rosalind under Webster at the Haymarket, with
James Anderson (who was to produce the play during
his disastrous tenancy of Drury Lane in 1850) as Jaques;
and Charlotte Cushman at the Princess's. In 1848,
under Mrs Warner, two other prominent Americans,
Davenport and Mrs Mowatt, act the play at the
Theatre Royal, Marylebone. Charles Kean stages it
with conscientious completeness at the Princess's in
1851. Barry Sullivan plays Jaques at the Haymarket
in 1855; and next year Miss Booth is there as Rosalind.
Phelps's production at Sadler's Wells was in 1857, and
he played Jaques. The list is far too long to give in full.
Let us leap to 1875, when the comedy is produced at the
Opera Comique, with Mrs Kendal as Rosalind, W. H.
Kendal as Orlando, Arthur Cecil as Touchstone, and
Hermann Vezin filling one of his many engagements
as Jaques. Ada Cavendish in 1878; Adelaide Neilson
in 1879; Miss Litton (with Lionel Brough for Touch-
stone) in 1880; the Kendals again at the St James's
Theatre in 1885, with their partner in management,
John Hare, as Touchstone, a pretty but pedantic pro-
duction by Lewis Wingfield and a newly arranged text;
Miss Wallis in 1888 (with Forbes-Robertson for
Orlando); Mrs Langtry, for the second time in 1890, a
production worth mentioning, perhaps, for its inclusion
of the Masque of Hymen; George Alexander, with Miss
Julia Neilson for Rosalind, in 1896: so the story goes on.

That last date takes us beyond an important point
in the modern history of the play, which must be approached by way of the United States. In the continent
of North America, *As You Like It* was first acted on

July 14, 1786, under the Hallam-Henry management at the John Street Theatre, New York, with Mrs Kenna, newly come from England, as Rosalind. We find it again in 1794 in the second season of the theatre at Boston; and the Wignell-Reinagle Company played it at the Chestnut Street Theatre, New York, in 1794–5. In 1798 the new first Park Theatre, New York, opened with it. In 1856 Laura Keene acts Rosalind; during the eighteen-eighties Rose Coghlan is often seen, indoors and out-of-doors, in the part. And in 1889 Ada Rehan acts it for the first time at Daly's Theatre, New York. In the year before, another American actress, Miss Mary Anderson, had played the part at the Memorial Theatre, Stratford-upon-Avon—and had been made to sing the Cuckoo Song. When Daly's version of the play was shown at the Lyceum Theatre, London, in July 1890, it was found that this hardy improver of Shakespeare had restored the First Lord's speeches to their proper owner, and that Miss Rehan, enchanting Rosalind that she was, did not have to sing the Cuckoo Song. Other Americans who have acted the play in England are Mr E. H. Sothern and Miss Julia Marlowe, in 1907, the year in which Mr Oscar Asche produced it at His Majesty's Theatre. In 1911 Miss Phyllis Neilson-Terry chose it for her first appearance on the stage, and gave Miss Miriam Lewes the chance of setting her Celia beside Mrs Clive's; and in 1920 Mr Nigel Playfair, at the St James's Theatre, with Miss Athene Seyler for Rosalind, staged it and produced it with originality and a fine dramatic economy.

In this long and populous tale there is one great and obvious gap. Miss Ellen Terry has never played Rosalind. It may be counted among the lapses in Henry Irving's judgment that he did not take Squire Bancroft's advice (*The Bancrofts*, 1909, pp. 326–7) and put up the play, with himself as Touchstone. What a Rosalind, and what a Touchstone, were lost!

HAROLD CHILD.

GLOSSARY

Note. Where a pun or quibble is intended, the meanings are distinguished as (*a*) and (*b*)

ABUSED, deceived; 3. 5. 79

ADDRESSED, equipped, prepared; 5. 4. 153

ADVENTURE, accident, chance; 2. 4. 44

ALLOTTERY, assignment of a share (N.E.D. quotes no other instance); 1. 1. 68

AMAZE, confuse, bewilder; 1. 2. 102

ANATOMIZE, lit. dissect (surg.), lay open minutely, expose; 1. 1. 146; 2. 7. 56

ASPECT, (*a*) glance, (*b*) the favourable or unfavourable influence of a planet according to the old astrologers; 4. 3. 53

ATOMIES, motes, specks of dust in a sunbeam; 3. 2. 230; 3. 5. 13

ATONE, unite, come into unity or concord; 5. 4. 107

BACK-FRIEND, a pretended or false friend; here used of a person who comes upon one from behind (for the same jest see *Err.* 4. 2. 37); 3. 2. 159

BANDY (IN FACTION), give and take recriminations; 5. 1. 57

BANQUET, a light repast of fruit and wine, often served as dessert after supper; 2. 5. 60

BARBARY COCK-PIGEON, 'a fancy variety of pigeon, of black or dun colour originally introduced from Barbary' (N.E.D. 'barb' 2); 4. 1. 145

ASTINADO, a beating or cudgelling, esp. upon the soles of the feet; 5. 1. 56

BATLER, a kind of wooden club for 'battling' (v. N.E.D.) or beating clothes during the process of washing; 2. 4. 48

BEGGARLY, like a beggar; 2. 5. 27

BESTOW ONESELF, to acquit oneself, bear oneself (cf. *Two Gent.* 3. 1. 87); 4. 3. 86

BILL, advertisement, proclamation (cf. *Ado,* 1. 1. 36); 1. 2. 114

BLUE EYE, i.e. with dark circles round the eye as from sleeplessness or weeping; 3. 2. 365

BOB, lit. (i) trick, deception, (ii) sharp rap or blow with the fist; and so, by combining the two meanings, 'taunt, bitter jest, jibe' (N.E.D.); 2. 7. 55

BONNY. N.E.D. states 'it appears to have often had the sense: Of fine size, big (as a good quality),' and quotes Hooker 'bonny and strong enough unto any labours'; 2. 3. 8

BOTTOM, dell, valley; 4. 3. 78

BOUNDS (OF FEED), 'limits within which he had the rights of pasturage' (Aldis Wright). Presumably these rights were in respect of the common land; 2. 4. 80; 3. 5. 107

BOW, a yoke for oxen; 3. 3. 75

BREATHED, exercised; 'well breathed' = put into good wind; 1. 2. 207

BREATHER, living being, creature (cf. *Son.* 81. 12; *Ant.* 3. 3. 24); 3. 2. 277

BUCKLE IN, encompass, limit; 3. 2. 132

BUGLE, i.e. black as bugle (=ornamental tube-shaped bead-work); 3. 5. 47

BUR, (a) prickly seed-vessel, (b) 'a bur in the throat' = anything that produced a choking sensation in the throat (N.E.D. 'bur' 4); 1. 3. 16

BURTHEN, accompaniment to a song, part for the bass; 3. 2. 245

BUSH, lit. 'a branch or bunch of ivy (perhaps as a plant sacred to Bacchus) hung up as a vintner's sign' (N.E.D.), and hence the tavern-sign itself; Ep. 3

BUTCHERY, slaughter-house, shambles; 2. 3. 27

CAGE OF RUSHES. A 'cage' was a lock-up for petty malefactors; 'a cage of rushes' would be a flimsy prison for a 'prizer' like Orlando; possibly, as Hart suggests, there is a side-glance at the rush-ring, commonly used for mock marriages among rustics (cf. *All's Well*, 2. 2. 24); 3. 2. 363

CAPABLE, either (i) passive, 'receivable,' or (ii) active, 'receptive, retaining'; 3. 5. 23

CAPON, a cock for eating. A 'capon-justice' was a 17th cent. term for a judge or magistrate bribed by gifts of capons (cf. N.E.D. 'capon'); 2. 7. 154

CARLOT, churl, peasant (N.E.D. quotes no other instance); 3. 5. 108

CAROL, orig. 'a ring-dance with song,' hence 'any kind of song sung at times of festival' (cf. *M.N.D.* 2. 1. 102); 5. 3. 27

CART, 'to cart with.' Bawds and harlots were punished by public exposure and whipping in a cart

drawn through the streets (cf. *Lear*, 4. 6. 165; *Shrew*, 1. 1. 55); 3. 2. 107

CAST, cast-off, discarded; 3. 4. 15

CHARACTER, engrave; 3. 2. 6

CHOPT, chapped; 2. 4. 49

CICATRICE, lit. 'the scar of a wound,' hence here 'a scar-like mark'; 3. 5. 23

CIVIL, variously interpreted as (i) grave or solemn, and (ii) civilised or refined; 3. 2. 128

CLAP INTO, 'to enter with alacrity and briskness upon anything' (Dr Johnson); 5. 3. 10

CLAP O'TH' SHOULDER, arrest (cf. *Err.* 4. 2. 37 'shoulder-clapper' = sergeant); 4. 1. 46

CODS, (a) pods, (b) testicles (cf. N.E.D. 'cod' 4); 2. 4. 51

COMBINE, bind (cf. *Meas.* 4. 3. 144 'I am combined by a sacred vow'); 5. 4. 147

COMFORTABLE, of good comfort, cheerful (cf. *Tim.* 3. 4. 71); 2. 6. 9

COMPACT OF, composed of. The word 'compact' also carries the meaning of 'tightly packed'; 2. 7. 5

CONCAVE, hollow (the orig. meaning); 3. 4. 23

CONCEIT, (i) fancy, imagination (cf. *Ham.* 3. 4. 114); 2. 6. 7; (ii) intelligence, mental capacity; 5. 2. 51

CONDUCT, leadership, command (of an army); 5. 4. 154

CONFINES, region, territory. No sense of 'confinement' intended; 2. 1. 24

CONSTANT (of a colour), uniform; 3. 5. 123

CONTRIVER, schemer, plotter; 1. 1. 136

CONVERTITE, a convert to a religious faith or way of life; 5. 4. 181

COPE, orig. 'to come to blows with, encounter in battle or tournament,' and so 'to hold converse or debate with' (cf. *Ham.* 3. 2. 60); 2. 1. 67

COPULATIVE, orig. a grammatical term; Touchstone, of course, means 'one about to be or desirous of being married'; 5. 4. 55

COUNTERCHECK, rebuke or rebuff (in retaliation for another). 'The figure is from the game of chess' (Ald. Wright); 5. 4. 79, 92

COVER, prepare the table, lay the cloth; 2. 5. 29

COVERED GOBLET. Goblets were generally fitted with ornamental covers, which were of course removed when the goblet was in use: a covered goblet was therefore an empty or 'concave' (q.v.) goblet; 3. 4. 24

CROSS, coin (der. from the practice of stamping one side of coins with the figure of a cross: cf. *L.L.L.* 1. 2. 32–33); 2. 4. 12

CURTLE-AXE. 'A much perverted form of the word "cutlass"' (N.E.D.); a heavy sword for cutting or slashing; 1. 3. 117

DAMASK, the colour of the damask rose, i.e. a blush-colour (cf. *Son.* 130. 5); 3. 5. 123

DEFY, reject, disdain; Ep. 18

DEVICE, invention, ingenuity; 1. 1. 156

DIAL. 'The allusion here may be either to a watch, or to a portable journey-ring or small sun-dial' (Halliwell). Aldis Wright compares *Ric. II*, 5. 5. 53–6;

1 *Hen. IV*, 5. 2. 84, both of which passages speak of the 'dial's point,' and therefore refer to watches or clocks; 2. 7. 20

DISABLE, disparage, belittle; 4. 1. 32; 5. 4. 75

DISCOVERY, (*a*) disclosure, (*b*) exploration (v. N.E.D. 'discovery' 3 *b*); 3. 2. 197

DISHONEST, (*a*) discreditable, (*b*) immodest, unchaste; 5. 3. 4

DISLIKE, express aversion to; 5. 4. 69

DISPUTABLE, disputatious; 2. 5. 33

DITTY, 'the words of a song, as distinguished from the music or tune' (N.E.D.); 5. 3. 40

DIVERTED BLOOD, i.e. 'blood diverted from the course of nature' (Dr Johnson). Shakespeare is using technical medical language; the old doctors professed to be able to 'divert' the course of the humours or the blood by means of medicinal appliances (v. N.E.D. 'diversion' 1 *b*); 2. 3. 37

DOG-APE, 'a dog-faced baboon' (Dyce). Aldis Wright quotes Chapman, *Humorous Day's Mirth*: 'So long as the compliments of a gentleman last, he is your complete ape'; 2. 5. 25

DOUBLET-AND-HOSE, the male attire of the period; we should say 'a man's suit'; 2. 4. 7; 3. 2. 195

DROP FORTH, bring forth; 3. 2. 235; 4. 3. 34

DRY BRAIN. 'In the physiology of Shakespeare's time a dry brain accompanied slowness of apprehension and a retentive memory' (Wright, who quotes *Batman vppon Bartholome*: 'He that hath such a braine receiueth slowly the feeling and printing

of thinges: but neverthelesse
when hee hath taken and re-
ceiued them, he keepeth them
long in mind'); 2. 7. 39

EFFIGIES, likeness, portrait; 2. 7.
196

EMBOSSED, swollen, tumid; 2. 7. 67

ENCHANTINGLY, 'as if under the
influence of a charm' (Wright);
1. 1. 157

ENGAGE, pledge; 5. 4. 163

EREWHILE, a little while back; 2. 4.
86; 3. 5. 105

ESTATE, bestow as an estate upon
(cf. *M.N.D.* 1. 1. 98); 5. 2. 11

EXERCISE, 'such exercises as may
become a gentleman,' i.e. the
occupations necessary for the
training of a young gentleman
(cf. *Two Gent.* 1. 3. 30–3); 1. 1.
67

EXPEDIENTLY, expeditiously,
promptly (N.E.D. quotes no
other instance of this sense); 3.
1. 18

EXTENT, seizure of lands in execu-
tion of a writ, sequestration; 3.
1. 17

EYNE, an old form of 'eyes,' rarely
used by the Elizabethans except
for rhyming purposes; 4. 3. 50

FACTION, dissension, factious
quarrel (v. *bandy*); 5. 1. 57

FALSE GALLOP, canter. Touchstone
quibbles (cf. note 3. 2. 96–7);
3. 2. 112

FANCY, love (of a not too serious
kind); 3. 5. 29

FANCY-MONGER, one who deals in
love; Orlando has filled the
forest with advertisements; 3.
2. 356

FANTASY, imagination (cf. *M.N.D.*
5. 1. 7–8); 2. 4. 30; 5. 2. 90

FAVOUR, appearance, face; 4. 3. 86;
5. 4. 27

FEATURES. If the word be taken
in the old-fashioned sense of
'limbs' or 'parts of the body'
(v. N.E.D. 'feature' 2 *b*), it will
be seen that Audrey had a touch
of Widow Wadman about her;
3. 3. 4

FEEDER, shepherd [or servant]; 2.
4. 96

FELL, the hide of an animal with
the wool or hair; 3. 2. 51

FLEET, to while away the time, to
let the time glide away. The
word is connected with 'float'
(v. N.E.D. 'fleet' v.^{1} 10 *d*); 1. 1.
112

FLUX, (i) continuous stream; 2. 1.
52; (ii) discharge from the
body; 3. 2. 65

FOIL, to throw (in wrestling); 1.
1. 123; 1. 2. 177; 2. 2. 14

FOND TO (with *inf.*), eager to, glad
to (v. N.E.D. 'fond' A 7); 2.
3. 7

FOOL (POOR), i.e. 'poor dear.'
Shakespeare often uses 'fool'
as a term of endearment or pity;
2. 1. 22, 40

FORKED HEADS, i.e. arrows. There
were two sorts of pointed
arrow: one with the points
looking backward and called the
broad-headed or swallow-tail,
the other with the points
stretching forward and called
the fork-headed or barbed. (See
Ascham, *Toxophilus*, ed. Arber,
pp. 135, 136); 2. 1. 24

FREESTONE-COLOURED, i.e. with
the dirty white or grey colour
of limestone; 4. 3. 25

GAMESTER, (*a*) athlete (N.E.D.
quotes from 1601, 'professed

wrestlers, runners and such gamesters at feats of activity'); (*b*) merry, frolicsome person; 1. 1. 153

GARGANTUA, the name of the voracious giant in Rabelais, who possessed so large a mouth that he swallowed five pilgrims, with their staves, in a salad; 3. 2. 223

GESTURE, bearing, manner; 5. 2. 60

GOD BUY YOU, the Elizabethan half-way house between 'God be with you' and the modern 'good-bye'; 3. 2. 255; 4. 1. 29; 5. 3. 45

GOD'ILD YOU, i.e. God yield you (where 'yield' = reward, repay) —'a common expression of gratitude or goodwill' (N.E.D.), though becoming archaic in the 17th cent.; 3. 3. 71; 5. 4. 53

GRAFF, an archaic variant of 'graft'; 3. 2. 117

GRAVELLED, perplexed, nonplussed (der. from 'gravelled' = run aground); 4. 1. 71

GREEK, in reference to the sb. meaning 'a cunning or wily person; a cheat, sharper, esp. one who cheats at cards' (N.E.D. sb. 4); 2. 5. 57

GROW UPON, (*a*) increase (or grow up) so as to become more troublesome, (*b*) take liberties with, presume upon; 1. 1. 81

HARD, with an uneasy pace. Onions quotes Holme's *Armony*, 1688, 'a Trotting horse, when he sets hard, and goes of an uneasy pace'; 3. 2. 310

HAVING, possession, property; 3. 2. 369

HEADED, i.e. come to a head, like a boil; 2. 7. 67

HEY-HO. 'An utterance apparently of nautical origin, and marking the rhythm of movement in heaving or hauling; often used in the burdens of songs with various emotional expression, according to intonation' (N.E.D.); 2. 7. 180, etc.

HIND, farm-servant; 1. 1. 18

HOLY BREAD, 'the (ordinary leavened) bread which was blessed after the Eucharist and distributed to those who had not communicated...the eulogia of the Greek Church and the French *pain bénit*' (N.E.D.); 3. 4. 14

HONEST, chaste; 1. 2. 36; 3. 3. 15, 23, 25, 31

HOOP, shout with astonishment (cf. *Hen. V*, 2. 2. 108); 3. 2. 193

HUMOROUS, moody; 1. 2. 254

HURTLING, noise of an encounter, collision or battle; 4. 3. 131

HYEN, hyena; 4. 1. 150

ILL-FAVOUREDLY, in an ugly fashion; 1. 2. 37

IMPRESSURE, impression (cf. *Tw. Nt.* 2. 5. 103); 3. 5. 23

INCISION, engrafting. 'In the 17th century,' N.E.D. tells us, 'incision' was 'often erroneously used for "insition," engrafting' ('incision' 5); 3. 2. 69

INCONTINENT, (*a*) straightway, (*b*) unchaste; 5. 2. 37

INDIRECT, wrong, unjust; 1. 1. 143

INLAND, belonging to the districts lying near the capital as opposed to the remote or outlying wild parts (v. N.E.D. 'inland' A3, B1 *b*); 2. 7. 96; 3. 2. 340

INSINUATE, ingratiate oneself with (cf. Marlowe, *Massacre of Paris*, 2. 4. 'Now, Madam, must you insinuate with the King'); Ep. 8

INSTANCE, illustration, example, proof; 2. 7. 156; 3. 2. 49, 54, 58

INSULT, triumph in an insolent fashion; 3. 5. 36

INTENDMENT, intention, project; 1. 1. 126

IRK, distress, pain; 2. 1. 22

JUST, exactly so. An expression of assent; the word 'quite' is often used to-day colloquially in much the same sense; 3. 2. 262

KIND, (i) sex (cf. *M. of V.* 1. 3. 82); 3. 2. 102; (ii) nature, character, inclination; 4. 3. 59

KINDLE, give birth to (generally used of hares and rabbits); 3. 2. 335

KINDNESS, natural instinct; 4. 3. 128

LEER, (*a*) face, complexion (a poetical word), (*b*) ogle; 4. 1. 64

LINE, (i) delineate, sketch; 3. 2. 90; (ii) Cf. Cotgrave, 1611: *Ligner*, To line, as a dog (or dog-wolf) a bitch; 3. 2. 104

LITTLE (IN), in miniature (cf. *Ham.* 2. 2. 383 'his picture in little'). But here Shakespeare is referring to man, who is the microcosm or miniature of the universe (v. note); 3. 2. 140

LIVELY, lifelike (cf. *Tim.* 1. 1. 38); 5. 4. 27

LIVER, formerly considered the seat of the passions; 3. 2. 411

LIVING, real, actual (cf. *Oth.* 3. 3. 409 'Give me a living reason she's disloyal'); 3. 2. 408

LOOK, i.e. look for (cf. *M.W.W.* 4. 2. 75 'I will look some linen'); 2. 5. 31

LUSTY, gay, bright (of a colour); 3. 5. 121

MAKE (THE DOOR), shut, close, bar (cf. *Err.* 3. 1. 93); 4. 1. 156

MANAGE, the action and paces to which a horse is trained when broken in; 1. 1. 12

MANNERS, (*a*) polite behaviour, (*b*) in the older sense of 'moral character' (cf. *M. of V.* 2. 3. 19 'Though I am daughter to his blood,/I am not to his manners'); 3. 2. 39, 40

MATERIAL, (*a*) 'stocked with notions' (Johnson; cf. *matter*); (*b*) gross, carnal (cf. N.E.D. 'material' 4*b*); 3. 3. 29

MATTER, topics for discussion or conversation; 2. 1. 68; 4. 1. 71; 5. 4. 182

MEASURE, a solemn dance, 'full of state and ancientry' (*Ado*, 2. 1. 69); 5. 4. 43, 176, 190

MEWL, mew like a cat. Cf. Cotgrave, 1611: '*Miauler*, to mewle, or mew, like a cat.' Because the word has only survived in modern times through Shakespeare's influence, it has come to mean 'whimper like an infant,' but Jaques was deliberately making comparison with cats; 2. 7. 144

MISPRIZE, fail to appreciate; 1. 1. 159

MISUSE, abuse, revile, misrepresent (cf. *Son.* 152. 7); 4. 1. 196

MO, more in number. Formerly 'more' = 'more in quantity' only; 3. 2. 259

MODERN, commonplace, trite; 2. 7. 156; 4. 1. 7

MOONISH, changeable, fickle; 3. 2. 400

MORALIZE, interpret, expound morally or symbolically; 2. 1. 44

MORTAL, (a) subject to death, (b) 'mortal in folly' = mortally foolish; 2. 4. 53, 54

MOTLEY. There were two sorts of fool at this period: the motley fool and the fool in the yellow petticoat. Apparently the motley fool was the superior intellectually, the other type being the 'natural' or idiot. The motley fool's costume consisted of a parti-coloured coat, with bells on the elbows or at the skirts; close hose and breeches, generally with the two legs of a different colour; and a hood decorated with asses' ears or cockscomb. He usually carried in his hand the sceptre of his office, the bauble, which was a stick ornamented with a fool's head at the end, to which was often attached the inflated bladder for the purpose of belabouring his enemies. Some fools carried a dagger of lath as well or instead. (Douce, *Illustrations of Shakespeare*, ii. 317); 2. 7. 13, 17, 29, etc.

NAMES. The general sense is clear (v. note), though the precise meaning is uncertain. Furness quotes from Cooper's *Thesaurus*, 1573, the best-known dictionary of the day, '*nomina*, the names of debtes owen'; 2. 5. 20

NATURAL, idiot; 1. 2. 50

NATURAL PHILOSOPHER, (a) scientist, esp. physicist, (b) Touchstone also glances at 'natural' = idiot, whose philosophy would be profound; 3. 2. 30

NAUGHT, (i) worthless, useless; 1. 2. 62; 3. 2. 15; (ii) 'be naught,' i.e. keep quiet, shut up, make yourself scarce; 1. 1. 33

NEW-FANGLED, carried away by novelty, giddy-pated; 4. 1. 147

OBSERVANCE, respectful attention; 3. 2. 232; 5. 2. 92

OCCASION, 'an opportunity of attacking, of fault-finding, of giving or taking offence; a "handle" against a person' (N.E.D. 'occasion' I. 1); 4. 1. 169

ODDS, superiority, advantage (cf. *L.L.L.* 1. 2. 169); 1. 2. 148

PAINTED CLOTH, the commonest and cheapest kind of wall-hanging, generally representing some tale or sentimental theme —'a pretty slight drollery, or the story of the Prodigal, or the German hunting in waterwork' (2 *Hen. IV*, 2. 1. 156–58)—with verses to match; 3. 2. 271

PAIR OF STAIRS, a flight of stairs ('pair' = set); 5. 2. 36

PANCAKE. The word 'pancake' in the 16th and 17th cent. was equivalent to 'fritter' or 'flapjack'; N.E.D. ('fritter' sb. 1) quotes Taylor the Water-Poet (1634): 'pancake or fritter or flapiacke.' Now meat-fritters might very well be eaten with mustard; 1. 2. 60

PANTALOON, orig. a stock figure of the Italian comic stage, representing Venice, and shown as a lean, foolish and vicious old man, wearing spectacles, hose and slippers (v. N.E.D. 'pantaloon' 1 a); hence 'a dotard; an old fool'; 2. 7. 158

PARCELS (IN), in detail, piece-meal; 3. 5. 124

PART, depart from; 2. 1. 51

PATHETICAL, passion-moving; 4. 1. 187

PLACES, texts, extracts, short passages from books (v. N.E.D. 7 *b*). The word can also mean 'topics or subjects of discourse,' which is the sense generally accepted; but this does not suit so well with 'vents in mangled forms'; 2. 7. 40

POINT-DEVICE, perfectly correct, very precise; 3. 2. 373

POLITIC, cunning, scheming; 5. 4. 44

PRACTICE, plot; 2. 3. 26

PRESENTATION, semblance; 5. 4. 104

PRIME, (*a*) spring-time, (*b*) the choicest quality; 5. 3. 35

PRINT (IN), precisely—with a quibble upon the orig. meaning; 5. 4. 88

PRIZER, prize-fighter; 2. 3. 8

PROFIT, progress in learning (cf. *Temp.* 1. 2. 172 'Have I, thy schoolmaster, made thee more profit'); 1. 1. 6

PROPER, handsome; 1. 2. 112; 3. 5. 51, 115

PUNY, lit. junior, hence 'a puny tilter'=a young or inexperienced. tilter; 3. 4. 41

PUKE, vomit; 2. 7. 144

PURCHASE, acquire; 3. 2. 337

PURGATION, (*a*) theol. 'clearing from guilt,' (*b*) medicinal purging; 1. 3. 53; 5. 4. 43

PURLIEU, 'a piece or tract of land on the fringe or border of a forest' (N.E.D.). This is the orig. meaning of the word; 4. 3. 76

PUT ON, pass off (something unwelcome) upon a person, force something upon one; 1. 2. 88

PYTHAGORAS, the Greek philosopher who preached the doctrine of the transmigration of souls; 3. 2. 177

QUAIL, slacken, become feeble (the orig. sense); 2. 2. 20

QUESTION, talk, conversation (a common meaning with Shakespeare; cf. *unquestionable*); 3. 4. 34; 5. 4. 158

QUINTAIN, a wooden figure at which to tilt. 'It was generally made in the likeness of a Turk or Saracen, armed at all points, bearing a shield upon his left arm, and brandishing a club or sabre with his right' (Strutt, *Sports and Pastimes*); 1. 2. 239

QUINTESSENCE, 'the "fifth essence" of ancient and mediaeval philosophy, supposed to be the substance of which the heavenly bodies were composed, and to be actually latent in all things, the extraction of it by distillation or other methods being one of the great objects of alchemy' (N.E.D.); 3. 2. 139

QUIP, sharp retort, sarcastic remark; 5. 4. 74, 91

QUOTIDIAN, a continuous fever or ague, as distinguished from the intermittent kinds; 3. 2. 357

RANKNESS, luxuriance of growth; 1. 1. 82

RASCAL, rabble, often used as a collective term for 'the young, lean or inferior deer of a herd, distinguished from the full-grown antlered bucks or stags' (N.E.D.); but Shakespeare appears to have used the term in the unusual sense of 'a deer with a great head and a small body, who would neither fight

nor run' (cf. *Cor.* I. I. 163 and
Sh. Eng. ii. 339 *n.*); 3. 3. 54

RECOUNTMENT, relation, recital·
(N.E.D. quotes no other instance); 4. 3. 140

RELIGIOUS, i.e. member ·of a religious order; 3. 2. 339; 5. 4.
157

RELISH, make pleasant to the
palate (e.g. by adding sauce); 3.
2. 232

REMORSE, pity, compassion; I. 3. 70

ROYNISH, scurvy, base; 2. 2. 8

SAD, serious; 3. 2. 212

SALE-WORK, 'ready-made goods'
(Wright); N.E.D. quotes 1775
Ash, *Saleswork*, work done for
sales, work slightly performed;
3. 5. 43

SCHOOL, university; I. I. 5

SCRIP, (*a*) wallet or satchel, such
as shepherds, beggars and fools
wore, (*b*) small piece of paper
(perhaps the usual term for
stage-paper; cf. *M.N.D.* I. 2. 3
'according to the scrip'); 3. 2.
163

SEAL up, make up (one's mind); 4.
3. 58

SEARCH (A WOUND), probe; 2. 4. 43

SEEMING, seemly; 5. 4. 68

SEIZE, take possession of according
to legal procedure; 3. I. 10

SENTENTIOUS, full of pithy sayings;
5. 4. 62

SEQUESTERED, excommunicated, cut
off from one's fellows; 2. I. 33

SHAKE UP, rate soundly, abuse
violently ('very common in the
16–17th cent.' N.E.D.); I. I. 26

SIMPLE, ingredient in medicine
(not necessarily a herb, though
by a natural process the word
came to be identified with that
sense); 4. I. 16

SIR ('Sir Oliver Martext'). This
title was commonly prefixed to·
the Christian names of ordinary
priests in medieval times, but
later came to be used in contrast to 'Master' and denoted
a priest or minister who had
not graduated at the university
(v. N.E.D. 'sir' 4 and *Sh. Eng.*
i. 59); 3. 3. 40

SLUT, (*a*) slattern, (*b*) a loose
woman; 3. 3. 32–5

SMOTHER, the dense smoke produced by a fire without flame;
I. 2. 275

SORT, class, rank; I. I. 156

SPLEEN, impulse, waywardness;
4. I. 207

SQUAND'RING, stray, straggling,
lavishly distributed; 2. 7. 57

STALKING-HORSE, i.e. an old horse
or ox, or a canvas imitation of
the same, behind which the
fowler lurked so as to get close
up to the game (v. *Sh. Eng.* ii.
372 for an excellent illustration
of 'stalking'); 5. 4. 103

STANZO, stanza. The word, a new
importation, seems to have
been regarded as affected by
Shakespeare, who puts it into
the mouth of Holofernes in
L.L.L. (4. 2. 110); 2. 5. 17

STING, sexual appetite; 2. 7. 66

SUN ('to live i'th' sun'). Usually
interpreted 'to live a free open-
air life,' but *Ham.* I. 2. 67 'I
am too much i'th' sun' suggests
a less obvious meaning. N.E.D.
connects it with the proverbial
phrase 'out of God's blessing
into the warm sun,' which referring originally no doubt to
the passing of a congregation
out of church, came to denote
·any change for the worse in

one's condition. The idea of outlawry, exclusion from society, would readily attach itself to the phrase, and would suit both contexts excellently. We interpret it therefore as 'to live the life of an outlaw'; 2. 5. 37

SWASHING, swaggering, dashing; 1. 3. 120

SWAY, control (in the astrological sense); 3. 2. 4

TAKE UP (A QUARREL), make up, settle; 5. 4. 47, 96

TAX, censure, blame; 2. 7. 71, 86; 3. 2. 344

TAXATION, satire, censure; 1. 2. 79

TEMPER, compound, mix, 'blend together the ingredients of a compound' (Wright); 1. 2. 11

TENDER, regard, value; 5. 2. 67

THRASONICAL, boastful, like Thraso the braggart soldier in Terence's *Eunuchus*; 5. 2. 30

TOUCH (i.e. with the pencil or brush), trait; 3. 2. 152; 5. 4. 27

TOUCHED, tainted; 3. 2. 343

TOY, trifle; 3. 3. 73

TURN, fashion or shape a work of art, a poem, a tune or a compliment; 2. 5. 3

TURN INTO, bring into; 4. 3. 23

UMBER, a brown earth used as a pigment; 1. 3. 112

UNBANDED, without a hatband; 3. 2. 370

UNDERHAND, quiet, not obvious, unobtrusive; 1. 1. 132

UNEXPRESSIVE, not to be expressed; 3. 2. 10

UNQUESTIONABLE, taciturn, averse to conversation (N.E.D. explains as 'not submitting to question, impatient,' but cf. *question* and *Ham.* 1. 4. 43 'questionable'); 3. 2. 366

USE, profit, benefit; 2. 1. 12

VENGEANCE, mischief, harm; 4. 3. 48

WARE, (*a*) aware, (*b*) cautious; 2. 4. 55, 56

WARP, (*a*) cause to shrink or corrugate; 2. 7. 187; (*b*) go astray from the straight path; 3. 3. 83

WEARING, wearying (cf. *All's Well*, '5. 1. 4); 2. 4. 37

WELL SAID! well done! 2. 6. 14

WORKING, endeavour; 1. 2. 192

WRATH OF LOVE, violent passion, ecstasy of love; 5. 2. 38

ADDENDA

ALLY, Kinsman; 5. 4. 181

CRY OUT ON, denounce; 2. 7. 7c

FANG, grip; 2. 1. 6

FRIEND, relative, ancestor; 1. 3. 62

RENDER, report; 4. 3. 122

SOUTH, S.W. wind; 3. 5. 50

WOMAN OF THE WORLD, married woman; 5. 3. 4

ORLAND PARK
PUBLIC LIBRARY
A Natural Connection

14921 Ravinia Avenue
Orland Park, IL 60462

708-428-5100
orlandparklibrary.org